Discipleship Preaching

A BIBLICAL PATTERN FOR PASTORS

Dr. Rob Finley

Master Design Publishing
FULTON, KENTUCKY

Copyright © 2020 by Prayer Resources, Inc.

All rights reserved. No part of this publication may be reproduced, distributed or transmitted in any form or by any means, including photocopying, recording, or other electronic or mechanical methods, without the prior written permission of the publisher, except in the case of brief quotations embodied in critical reviews and certain other noncommercial uses permitted by copyright law.

Published by Prayer Resources in cooperation with
 Master Design Publishing
 an imprint of Master Design Marketing, LLC
      789 State Route 94 E
      Fulton, KY 42041
      MasterDesign.org

Cover and interior design by Faithe Thomas
Photos/Images © DepositPhotos.com

Ordering Information:
Special discounts are available on quantity purchases. For details, contact Prayer Resources (see info in back of book).

Unless indicated otherwise, all Scripture quoted in this book is from the *King James Version of the Bible*, and is Public Domain.

Scripture marked Weymouth is from the *Weymouth New Testament in Modern Speech*, Third Edition 1913, and is Public Domain.

Scripture marked NASB is from the NEW AMERICAN STANDARD BIBLE®, Copyright © 1960, 1962, 1963, 1968, 1971, 1972, 1973, 1975, 1977, 1995 by The Lockman Foundation. Used by permission.

Print ISBN: 978-1-941512-44-9
Ebook ISBN: 978-1-941512-45-6
Printed in the USA

Contents

Dedication v

Acknowledgements vi

1: The Biblical Pattern for Discipleship 1

2: Salvation 11

3: Separation 31

4: Surrender... 41

5: Spirit-Control... 55

6: Suffering 79

7: Sensitivity.. 101

8: Spirituality 113

9: Conclusion 125

Resources... 145

About Prayer Resources 147

Dedication

This book is dedicated to three of God's choicest servants who have served as the Lord's tool to disciple me and to shape so much of the truth that is presented throughout the book. Others have impacted my life, but perhaps none as much as these three:

Carl William Wilson: Before Jesus issued the Great Commission to make disciples, He first trained disciple-builders. Carl Wilson's book, *With Christ in the School of Disciple Building*, has impacted my life in this craft of disciple building more than any one else. Thank you, Carl, for giving me the example of a Disciple Builder!

Stephen Frederick Olford: Stephen Olford's emphasis upon expository preaching of the text of the Word of God has greatly impacted my approach to preaching and writing. His model of anointed preaching continues to challenge me on a regular basis. Thank you, Stephen, for your example of an Expositor!

Leonard Ravenhill: Leonard Ravenhill's book, *Why Revivals Tarries*, had and continues to have a profound impact upon my life as a revivalist. He clarified for me the difference between the evangelist and evangelism AND the revivalist and revivalism. Thank you, Leonard, for giving me the example of a true Revivalist!

May there be rejoicing in Heaven as the message built in your lives continues to challenge others!

Acknowledgements

Discipleship Preaching would never have come about if it were not for the diligent oversight and proof-reading of my wife of over 50 years, **Judy Staggers Finley**. Each page reflects her Biblical insights and prayerful comments. Thank you, Judy, for your partnership in this ministry.

Our older daughter, **Faithe Finley Thomas**, has polished, improved, and corrected more in this book than I would care to admit! Thank the Lord for your skillful proofing, counseling, and editing of this book.

*From the very instant of Creation
until we gather at the Throne of God,
there is orderliness everywhere.*

*Discovering God's pattern of discipleship
and applying that pattern to preaching
should be the hallmark of strong Biblical,
expository preaching.*

The Biblical Pattern for Discipleship

*Go therefore and **make disciples** of all the nations, baptizing them in the name of the Father and the Son and the Holy Spirit, teaching them to observe all that I commanded you; and lo, I am with you always, even to the end of the age.*
– Matthew 28:19, 20 NASB

CHAPTER 1

By God's grace and according to His good purposes, I began my days as a pastor with the firm conviction that the only direct command in the great commission is to make disciples. The baptizing and the teaching are merely activities to accomplish the goal to make disciples. But as the days turned into weeks, and the weeks into months, and the months into years, I began to realize that every program of discipleship that I had been taught was merely hit or miss teaching. I recognized my need for a plan with measurable goals that would bring my congregation to spiritual maturity. I desired a plan that would avoid the pride of knowledge and the competitive spirit of disunity. With a cry to the Lord, I made my way to the local Christian bookstore – the Siri of my day. As I perused the discipleship shelf filled with books that were already on my shelves at home, I came across the book that would set me on a path that would shape both my life and my discipling method. The book's title intrigued me: *With Christ in the School of Disciple Building*. Its author is Carl Wilson who had been used of the Lord in work with both Billy Graham and Campus Crusade. He had recently started his own campus ministry with Worldwide Discipleship Association. Carl's thorough knowledge of the Gospels had allowed him to discover a distinct pattern that Jesus used in making His original twelve disciples. Jesus and the disciples employed the exact same pattern when they began to disciple the 70 and then again with the 120. When I began to apply Jesus' seven steps of discipleship with both the small group of men with whom I met in a more spiritually intimate setting and with my congregation through my preaching, I began to see spiritual growth in leaps and bounds comparable to the weeds in my front yard! I no longer had to struggle with where to go next in my preaching topics. I could easily determine the appropriate books of the Bible that would bring my congregation to the next step in their discipleship journey. I allowed the seven steps that Jesus had used to make disciples to govern my annual cycle of sermon topics.

Although no substitute for a thorough reading of the book *With Christ in the School of Disciple Building*, this summary chart will provide a quick overview of Carl Wilson's concepts:

Steps	Text	Ministry Focus	Related Doctrines	Topics Taught
Repentance/ Faith	Mark 1:1-13	Preaching of John & Jesus, Baptism, Temptation	*Justification*	God, Man, Satan, Creation, Gospel, Repentance, Assurance
Enlightenment	John 1-4	Call of early disciples, healings, miracles	*Regeneration*	Sin, Temptation, Baptism, Morality, Witnessing, Separation
Ministry Training	Mark 1:14-3:21	Calling of Twelve, Sermon on Mount, Parable Teaching	*Lordship of Christ*	Stewardship, Tithe, Prayer, Ambitions, God's Will, Relationships
Leadership Development	Mark 3:22-6:29	Rejection at Nazareth, Commission of Twelve, Death of John the Baptist	*Trinity, Holy Spirit*	Sovereignty of God, Gifts of Spirit, Service, Prophecy, Angels, Strongholds
Re-Evaluation	Mark 6:30-9:32	Discipleship Truths, Transfiguration, Passion, Prophecy	*Perseverance*	Providence, Trust, Welfare, Sacrifice, Religious Liberty
Participation/ Delegation	Mark 9:33-10:31	Commission of 70, Marriage and Divorce	*Christian Works*	Church, Judaism, Kingdoms of God/Satan
Exchanged Life	Mark 10:32-16:20	Triumphal Entry, Upper Room, Crucifixion, Ascension	*Sanctification*	Fruitfulness, Love, Judgement, Death, Second Coming

My understanding of Jesus' seven steps of discipleship became even more fine-tuned when I discovered that Peter had presented the steps in clear terminology as he described the sequence of authentic Christianity in 2 Peter 1:3-7: *Whereby are given unto us exceeding great and precious promises: that by these ye might be partakers of the divine nature, having escaped the corruption that is in the world through lust. According as His divine power hath given unto us all things that pertain unto life and godliness, through the knowledge of Him that hath called us to glory and virtue: And beside this, giving all diligence, add to your faith virtue; and to virtue knowledge; And to knowledge temperance; and to temperance patience; and to patience godliness; And to godliness brotherly kindness; and to brotherly kindness charity.*

Not only did Peter list the steps of discipleship that Jesus had used to make disciples, but he also described the desperate consequences of not following these distinct steps. He contributed both the lack of fruit in the believer's life (v 8) and his doubts of his salvation (v 9) to a failure to follow these steps. Peter then challenged his readers to give diligence to make sure of their calling by following these steps (v 10).

Because I have found alliteration to be a great help to my memory, I began to assign alliterated words to this pattern of discipleship that seems to be repeated in Scripture. I also began to see specific Old Testament and New Testament books whose themes reflect the specific steps.

Assurances	Steps of Discipleship	OT Books	NT Books	Tension of Issues
Faith	**SALVATION**	Genesis	Gospels	Faith vs Works
Virtue	**SEPARATION**	Exod-Deut	Acts	Good vs Evil
Knowledge	**SURRENDER**	Josh-Ruth	Letters by Paul	Truth vs Error
Temperance	**SPIRIT-CONTROL**	1 Sam-2 Chr	Letters by James/Jude	Spirit vs Flesh
Patience/Godliness	**SUFFERING**	Ezra-Neh	Letters by Peter	Eternal vs Temporal
Brotherly Kindness	**SENSITIVITY**	Poetry/Wisdom	Letters by John	Light vs Darkness
Charity/Love	**SPIRITUALITY**	Prophets	Revelation	Holy vs Profane

Later while preparing to lead our family worship in celebration of the Passover, I discovered that God also had a discipleship pattern for His nation of Israel. He had instructed them through Moses to celebrate a series of seven distinct festivals at definite times throughout each year. God had provided them with an annual curriculum to bring them to spiritual maturity! Each feast had a spiritual purpose, and each of those purposes corresponded with the same pattern that Jesus used with His disciples and that Peter outlined in his sequence of authentic Christianity in 2 Peter 1:3-7!

Feast	Time	Meaning for Israel	Meaning for the Church	Fore-shadowed Event	Steps of Discipleship
Passover *pesah* Ex 12:1-28 Lev 23:5	1st Month 14th Day	Faith in the Blood of the Lamb to save the firstborn from death	Believer's faith in the Blood of Jesus to save from sin	Crucifixion	**Salvation**
Unleavened Bread *matsot* Ex 12:15-20 Lev 23:6-8	1st Month 15th-21st Day	Separation of leaven from home and food picturing purging of sin	Purging of the Believer's sin	Burial	**Separation**
First Fruits *bikkurim* Lev 23:9-14	1st Month 23rd Day	Sacrifical surrender of the first grain harvest in gratitude for saving firstborn	Jesus is surrendered from death as the first fruit of all who will be resurrected	Resurrection	**Surrender**
Pentecost *shavuot* Lev 23:15-22 Num 28:26-31	3rd Month 6th Day	The Spirit at Creation & the law to guide and empower Israel	The Spirit to guide and empower Believers throughout the Church Age	Church Age	**Spirit Control**
Trumpets *ros hashanah* Lev 23:23-25 Num 29:1-6	7th Month 1st Day	Sound to gather Israelites suffering in the wilderness	Sound at Church's rapture & onset of Great Tribulation	Rapture/Tribulation	**Suffering**
Atonement *yom kippur* Lev 16 Lev 23:26-32 Num 29:7-11	7th Month 10th Day	Increased sensitivity to sin & God's faithful forgiveness	The Lord's increased sensitivity to remove Israel's blindness	Return of the Lord	**Sensitivity**

Feast	Time	Meaning for Israel	Meaning for the Church	Fore-shadowed Event	Steps of Discipleship
Tabernacles *sukkoth* Lev 23:33-43 Num 29:12-38	7th Month 15th-22nd Day	Reminder of wilderness dwellings / peace and rest from the final harvest work	1000 year peaceful reign of Jesus when all nations will come to Jerusalem to worship and form their worldview	Millennial Reign	**Spirituality**

It is interesting to note that this Biblical pattern for discipleship is not just given in Scripture as specific steps, but it is also illustrated in the lives of individuals. Paul described each of the seven steps succinctly in his beautiful hymn of wonder at the magnificence of Christ in Philippians 2. As illustrated in this chart, the life of Jesus and of both Peter and Paul bear testimony to their having given all diligence to make their calling sure:

Steps of Discipleship	Jesus' Pattern	Peter's Pattern	Paul's Pattern
Salvation	*Who, being in the form of God, thought it not robbery to be equal with God* (Phil 2:6)	Call to Discipleship (Mtt 4:18-20)	Conversion (Acts 9:1-19; 22:1-16; 26:1-20)
Separation	*But made Himself of no reputation* (Phil 2:7a) Heb 7:26	Separation from Others (Lk 5:8; Mtt 10:2; 14:28; Mk 5:37)	Commission (Acts 9:6,10-18; Eph 3:1-8) Separated 3 years (Gal 1:15-18)
Surrender	*and took upon Him the form of a servant, and was made in the likeness of men* Is 50:4, Jn 6:45	Proclamations (Mtt 16:16; 17:1,4; 19:27; Jn 13:36-37) Denial (Mtt 26:72)	Surrender from old life (Phil 3:4-10; 1 Tim 1:12-16)

Steps of Discipleship	Jesus' Pattern	Peter's Pattern	Paul's Pattern
Spirit-Control	*And being found in fashion as a man, He humbled Himself* (Phil 2:8a) Lk 4:14,18; Acts 10:38; Jn 1:32	Pentecost (Acts 1:13,15; 2:4,17; 4:8)	Spirit's renewed call (Acts 13:1-4; 26:19-20)
Suffering	*and became obedient unto death* (Phil 2:8b) Heb 5:8; Lk 2:35	Imprisonment (Acts 4:13,21; 5:18,29; 12:3)	Various tribulations in missions (Acts 9:23-35; Gal 1:17; 2 Cor 11:32-33)
Sensitivity	*even the death of the cross* (Phil 2:8c) Lk 4:18; Mk 10:21	Reaching out to Brothers (Mtt 18:21; 1 Pet 1:22; 2 Pet 1:7; Acts 10:28; 1 Pet 3:8)	Follow-up Missionary Journeys (Acts 15:36-21:17) Maturity in Epistles (Eph, Phil, Col, 2 Tim)
Spirituality	*Wherefore God also hath highly exalted Him, and given Him a name which is above every name* (Phil 2:9) Jn 14:21; 15:9,12; Mtt 22:37-39	Love Commitment (Jn 21:15; 1 Pet 4:8; 5:14)	Emphasis upon Love (1 Cor 13:1-13)

These stated illustrations of the Lord's seven steps to make disciples of His people are merely scratching the surface of the number of times the pattern appears throughout the Scriptures. There is, indeed, a Biblical pattern for discipleship. I pray that this book will serve as a tool to establish the pattern in your own life and in the lives of those to whom you minister!

Salvation

embracing faith

Whereby are given unto us exceeding great and precious promises: that by these ye might be partakers of the divine nature, having escaped the corruption that is in the world through lust. According as His divine power hath given unto us all things that pertain unto life and godliness, through the knowledge of Him that hath called us to glory and virtue: And beside this, giving all diligence, add to your faith...
– 2 Peter 1:3-5a

CHAPTER 2

A Life-Message Initiated by Salvation

And Jesus went about all Galilee, teaching in their synagogues, and preaching the Gospel... – Matthew 4:23

To follow the Biblical pattern of discipleship in our preaching, we must begin where the Christian life begins: with saving faith! In order to preach effectively, our preaching should flow out of our relationship with God through intimate prayer. A foundational principle in preaching is this: *a message built in a life reaches a life; a message built merely in the mind reaches only a mind.*

Thus, we begin with God! The Bible begins with God – a unique Triune Creator! In Genesis 1:1-3, we are presented the key to unlocking the Scriptures, and that key is God the Father, God the Son, and God the Holy Spirit. Each of the Gospels begins with the Trinity! Virtually each of the New Testament epistles begins with the Trinity. So we too begin with the Trinity.

The preacher must develop a personal relationship with this Unique Being, for there is none like Him (Isaiah 45:21-22)! In examining the Trinity, we see that He is...

- **Veiled** in the Old Testament (Genesis 1:1-3; 1:26; 3:22; Deuteronomy 6:4; Isaiah 6:8)
- **Visible** in the New Testament (Romans 1:20; Colossians 1:9-10; Luke 3:21-22; 1 John 1:1-3)

- ☐ **Vital** within the Church (1 Peter 1:2; Ephesians 5:17-20)
- ☐ **Valuable** to the Believer (Isaiah 6:3,8; John 14:16,26; 2 Corinthians 13:14; John 15:26)

May God bless you as you establish a life-message **initiated by faith!**

What Moses Knew That Few Pastors Realize

*And He [the Lord] said, My **presence** shall go with thee, and I will give thee rest. And he [Moses] said unto Him, If Thy **presence** go not with me, carry us not up hence.*
— Exodus 33:14-15

Moses had experienced the unique **presence** of God at the burning bush and again at Mount Sinai. He had faithfully followed that same **presence** as symbolized in the pillar of fire and the pillar of cloud while journeying in the Wilderness.

In the text before us, Moses entered into the Tent of Meeting to come before the Lord *face to face* [could be translated, *presence to presence*] as a man speaks unto his friend. God then commissioned Moses to continue to lead the people of Israel to the Promise Land. When the meeting drew to a close, Moses turned to the Lord and sought the assurance that His unique **manifest presence** would go with him before the Children of Israel.

Moses knew that just presenting the truths of God was insufficient. His greater assignment was to present God's **manifest presence** to the people of God. Let us not come short of that assignment. We must bring God's **manifest presence** to the people of God – that same **manifest presence** that we have come to know at the time of our salvation and our calling, in revival, and in our devotions! May our sermons drip with that **manifest presence!**

The God Everyone Should Know

> *...that thou mayest know that there is none like unto the LORD our God.* – Exodus 8:10

We are commissioned to stand before this world, even as Moses stood before Pharaoh, and proclaim that there is no God like unto this Lord God! All gods are not the same! The God Who revealed Himself to Moses is not like any other god!

God revealed Himself to Moses by the name of **God** (*Elohim*) – the all-knowing God Who creates all things according to His purposes. In Exodus 3:6, He said, *I am the God (Elohim) of thy father, the God of Abraham, the God of Isaac, and the God of Jacob.*

God also revealed Himself to Moses by the name of **Lord** (*Adonai*) – the all-powerful Lord Who controls His creation by His power. In Exodus 4:13 *O my Lord (Adonai), send, I pray Thee, by the hand of him whom Thou wilt send.*

God further revealed Himself to Moses by the name of **Holy One** (*Kadosh*) – the totally-righteous God Who convicts and converts by His purity. In Exodus 3:5 *and He said, Draw not nigh hither: put off thy shoes from off thy feet, for the place whereon thou standest is holy (Kadosh) ground.*

Lastly, God revealed Himself to Moses by the name of **LORD** (*Yahweh* or *Jehovah*) – the ever-present LORD Who covenants with believers through His presence! Exodus 3:2 *And the angel of the LORD (Yahweh/Jehovah) appeared unto him in a flame of fire...*

When we consider the four names of our God as revealed to Moses, we find them amplified elsewhere in Psalms 78, 89, 139, 107, and Isaiah 40. This God is like no other! We are to present this Lord God before our people! May I ask, is this the God you preach?

> *I am the* LORD, *and there is none else, there is no God beside Me.*   *– Isaiah 45:5*

Longing for God's Manifest Presence

> *...my heart and my flesh crieth out for the living God.*
>   *– Psalm 84:2b*

The Psalmist longed for the Lord's presence...once again! He reflected back upon those special times in his life when he sensed God's presence being more real than his own! Let us be challenged by Psalm 84, to examine those times and places where we too have been refreshed by God's presence.

First, the Psalmist considers the **Sacred Places** (Psalm 84:1-2). God's presence resides in His tabernacles or dwelling places! Locations where God has come down in the midst of His people have continued to be marked by His presence. The Psalmist suggests places such as the Temple, the Wailing Wall in Jerusalem, sanctuaries where revival took place, or perhaps special services (such as a wedding, a laying on of hands, baptism, commissioning, etc.).

Second, the Psalmist considers the **Special Altars** (Psalm 84:3). How special are those kneeling rails and mourner benches upon which revival, a rededication, or a conversion took place. How special are those moving invitations in a crusade or the prayer altars in a church's prayer room. To once again revisit those altars is to sense God's presence once again.

Third, the Psalmist considers the **Suffering People** (Psalm 84:4-7). Those who have passed through the valley of Baca (lit. weeping) provide opportunities for us to experience God's presence. Through those who have suffered or have experienced God in a deeper way than we have, God's presence becomes so real! Their suffering, their pilgrimage, their walk with the Lord somehow moves us from strength to strength as we sense God's presence in them! God wants His ministers to get out among the people and to empathize with them – and, more importantly, to sense God's manifest presence in them!

Fourth, the Psalmist considers the **Specific Prayers** (Psalm 84:4,9). God's presence is sensed through our prayers or the prayers of others. We could reflect back upon praying with a godly individual, or a cottage prayer meeting for revival, or the prayers of dedication at a baby dedication or a wedding. Or perhaps we recall those deep prayers when we cried out to God to intervene! How often our prayers have brought us into His presence!

Fifth, the Psalmist considers the **Selected Mentors** (Psalm 84:10). There have been times when we have been drawn into God's presence by those through whom God has worked mightily in times past. These Spirit-filled servants have made us aware of God's presence! We reflect back upon those encounters in which they were conduits for God's presence!

Sixth, the Psalmist considers the **Servant Opportunities** (Psalm 84:10). Humbling service, as illustrated by the activities of a doorkeeper at the Temple, suggests that we experience God's presence as we humbly serve. This act of service may include praying with a dying saint, taking food to a dear shut-in, giving to a special offering, giving money to a homeless person, or going on a mission trip. God uses these humble acts of service to draw us near to Himself.

Lastly, the Psalmist considers the **Scheduled Times** (Psalm 84:11). From our daily quiet times to the times of temptation to the times of testing, we experience God's provisions and protections through the closeness of His presence! Those times may simply be a providential encounter or a challenging stepping out in faith! Indeed, those times are precious as we experience the very presence of God!

The Psalmist closes Psalm 84 with the challenge to trust in the Lord at all times, to walk uprightly with integrity, and to seek opportunities to experience God afresh.

The Key That Unlocks All of Scripture

> *Hear, O Israel, The LORD our God is one LORD: And thou shalt love the LORD thy God with all thine heart, with all thy soul, and with all thy might.* – Deuteronomy 6:4-5

In years gone by, people used to hide the key to their front door under the doormat, above the door frame, or in a nearby plant. The key to the whole house was right there at the front door! Likewise, our Creator placed the key that unlocks the whole of Scripture right at the first, Genesis 1:1-3! That key is the Tri-unity (or Trinity) of God.

This key is amplified further throughout the Bible, but never so powerfully as found in Deuteronomy 6:4-5. Note the singular Lord and a plural designation of God accompanied by the singular verb "is"! Hidden right there in plain view for all to see is the Trinity! The Trinity Key unlocks the rest of Scripture.

- ☐ **God** is a trinity of Father, Son, and Holy Spirit (Genesis 1:1-3; 1:26; Deuteronomy 6:4)
- ☐ **Man** is a trinity of spirit, soul, and body (Hebrews 4:12, 16; 1 Thessalonians 5:23)
- ☐ **Rebellion** is a trinity of sin, transgression, and iniquity (1 John 2:16)
- ☐ **Salvation** is a trinity of God's grace, Man's faith, and the believer's witness (Ephesians 2:8-10; Matthew 28:19-20)

Many other truths are revealed as a trinity, yielding a balance of truth between two paradoxical other truths. Theological debates can be settled by realizing that the balance of truth is often found in the middle between two polarizing positions!

What the Trinity Is Not

> *Elect according to the foreknowledge of God the Father, through sanctification of the Spirit, unto obedience and sprinkling of the blood of Jesus Christ: Grace unto you and peace, be multiplied.*   – 1 Peter 1:2

We have been writing concerning the preacher's relationship to the Trinity. Let us pause and define what we mean by the term. ***The Trinity is a description of the Godhead in which the unique community of Divine Persons are co-essential, co-existent, co-eternal, and co-equal.***

One of the difficulties of staying in theological balance is holding truths in tension or tautness. There are at least six errors in regards to the study of the Trinity.

- **The Three-gods Error** – This false teaching, called *tritheism*, states that God is not one, but three gods! This polytheistic view is clearly rejected by the Early Church. (1 John 5:7)
- **The Other-modes of the Godhead Error** – This popular view, known as *modalism*, teaches that there is one God, but He appears in three different forms throughout history, but never at the same time. This view is also rejected by the Early Church. (Luke 3:21)
- **The Spirit-only Error** – This view places such excessive emphasis upon the Person of the Holy Spirit that He becomes tantamount as the only Person of the

Trinity. The Charismatic movement leans this direction. (John 15:26)
- **The Jesus-only Error** – This view places such excessive emphasis upon the Person of Jesus that He becomes tantamount as the only Person of the Trinity. Baptists lean this direction when prayers are voiced to Jesus instead of the Father or when they hold rallies proclaiming "just give me Jesus." (Luke 11:2)
- **The Father-only Error** – This view places such excessive emphasis upon the Father that He becomes tantamount as the only Person of the Trinity. Some Protestants focus primarily upon God the Father with little regard to a personal Savior and little recognition of the Spirit. (John 14:9)
- **The Other-persons of the Godhead Error** – This view places an excessive emphasis upon an historic person, such as Mary or one of the saints, that this person becomes tantamount to the level of a fourth person of the Godhead. (Jeremiah 10:6)

The grace of the Lord Jesus Christ, and the love of God, and the communion of the Holy Ghost, be with you all. Amen.
– 2 Corinthians 13:14

Praying That Every Pastor Is Saved

Now therefore arise, O LORD God, into Thy resting place, Thou, and the ark of Thy strength: let Thy priests, O LORD God, be clothed with salvation, and let Thy saints rejoice in goodness. *– 2 Chronicles 6:41*

Dr. Elmer Towns states in his book, *Praying the Lord's Prayer for Spiritual Breakthrough*, that a friend of his who is an Episcopal priest challenges his congregation each Sunday morning with these words: "I know God...and this morning at the worship service, you can know God. Then he offers an even greater challenge: This week I have touched God, and this morning you can touch God. But more importantly, God can touch you."

In this chapter, we have been considering the first step of applying the Biblical pattern of discipleship to your preaching, namely, **experiencing a life-message initiated by salvation**. The preacher must know God intimately and personally. He must experience *salvation*! A message built in a life will reach a life. A message merely built in the mind will reach only a mind.

And we must not take for granted that every preacher is saved. Many are not.

Pastor, your preaching will never rise above your relationship with God! Stated another way, you will go no further in producing eternal fruit than what your quiet time with the Lord will take you! We must proclaim God to the people so He can change them!

Our task in the pulpit is not to impress a congregation by our theological terminologies nor our polished pulpit skills. Our task is simple: humbly slip into the background and allow God to touch each person in attendance by His presence!

> *Now when they saw the boldness of Peter and John, and perceived that they were unlearned and ignorant men, they marveled; and took knowledge of them, that they had been with Jesus.*   – Acts 4:13

Blindsided

In my distress I cried to the LORD, And He heard me.
– Psalm 120:1

Psalm 120 marks the first of fifteen Psalms of Ascent most likely collected by King Hezekiah. These Psalms were utilized as hymns to be recited by pilgrims as they traveled up to Jerusalem for one of the three Jewish festivals.

This series of Psalms illustrates a zealous pilgrim beginning the exciting journey to worship God. Unexpectedly, the pilgrim is blindsided by lying lips and deceitful tongues from those whom he would least expect it – fellow pilgrims who have traveled from distant lands.

Many a preacher starts out with holy zeal only to be blindsided by fellow Christians, church leaders, or fellow preachers! Accusations fly at him like arrows! Slanderous words burn upon him like burning coals of fire! Wounded and burnt, the young preacher turns to the Lord Who always hears his prayers. While the slanderers always mean harm, God is shaping a peace-maker in the life of the preacher!

Note the Psalmist's thoughts: the Trials of a Holy Pursuit (vv 1,4-6), the Triumph of Holy Prayers (vv 2-4), and the Transformation of Holy Peace (vv 5-7). Building a life message into the ministry of the preacher often begins when holy zeal encounters hateful slander! The shaping of a minister of reconciliation must begin where Jesus began with us – with a forgiving heart!

Forgiving someone of hateful words may be the greatest sermon that we can ever preach! May we follow Jesus' example and pray, *Father, forgive them for they know not what they do!*

Balanced Preaching

Preach the Word; be instant in season, out of season; reprove, rebuke, exhort with all longsuffering and doctrine.
— 2 Timothy 4:2

The Apostle Paul described balance in this great verse on preaching. Balanced preaching should include a three-fold presentation, no matter the timing or the situation. This three-fold thrust should include **content** (*logos*), **credibility** (*ethos*), and **conviction** (*pathos*).

The Scriptures describe the preaching of Jesus and the Apostles with **concrete content** with words such as the *gospel* (Matthew 11:5), *repentance* and *remission of sins* (Luke 24:47), and *Christ* (Acts 8:5). Our preaching should be no less based on truth and logic!

In addition, the Scriptures describe the Apostles' preaching based on **credibility and believability** so as to persuade unbelievers (1 Corinthians 1:18, 23), to present them before the final Judge (Acts 10:42) and to preach for a decision (Acts 16:10). Often Paul would present his message with overwhelming support, as he did in 1 Corinthians 15, by testifying to the truth of the resurrection.

The Scriptures also describe preaching with **conviction** as expressed with the words such as *boldly* (Acts 9:27), *ready* (Acts 1:15), *warning* (Colossians 1:28) and *woe* (1 Corinthians 9:16). The Apostles spoke with passion and conviction. Jesus spoke of the strong persuasive preaching of John the Baptist. His own preaching was full of great compassion (Matthew 11:17; Luke 7:32).

Thus, taken as a whole, the Scriptures present Biblical preaching that is based upon logical content, ethical credibility, and passionate convictions. Such preaching is sadly lacking today!

> [Jesus said...] *What I tell you in darkness, that speak ye in light: and what ye hear in the ear, that preach ye upon the housetops.*
> – Matthew 10:27

The First Christian Sermon

> *But Peter, standing up with the eleven, lifted up his voice, and said unto them, Ye men of Judaea, and all ye that dwell at Jerusalem, be this known unto you, and hearken, to my words:*
> – Acts 2:14

Peter stood to preach the first Christian sermon. This sermon was critical, for it would establish the vision, foundation, and distinction of all subsequent Christian sermons! Today it should serve as the plumb line to measure our sermons. It is worth our time to examine Peter's sermon thoughts.

A. **The Promise of the Holy Spirit of God** (Acts 2:16-21) The Age of the Spirit had come, and the starting place was in this sermon! Peter spoke of the significance of the Spirit in answer to Jesus' ascension prayer, the signal that the Messiah had truly come, and the sign of His filling upon the disciples! All Christian preaching should be Spirit-anointed. Peter boldly proclaimed that whoever would call upon the Name of the Lord would be saved. This truly is the work of the Spirit!

B. **The Passion of the Messiah Jesus of Nazareth** (Acts 2:22-24) Peter focused his sermon upon Jesus! He preached about Jesus' life and ministry, about the crucifixion, and the resurrection. These themes are what is called the Passion of Christ. In other words, he focused upon the death, burial, and resurrection of Jesus!

C. **The Prophecy of King David of Israel** (Acts 2:25-31) Then Peter validated his message with the references to significant Biblical prophecies that Jesus fulfilled. He is the heir to David's throne and the Messiah to the Jews!

D. **The Proclamation by Himself Concerning the Eleven** (Acts 2:32-36) Peter spoke about the Spirit's coming upon the Eleven as evidence that He was sent by Jesus Who is both Lord and Christ! God foreknew, Joel foretold, and David foresaw that Jesus is the hope of Israel!

Conclusion (Acts 2:37-40) Peter drew in the net when he preached repentance, baptism because of the remission of sins, and receiving the promised Holy Spirit.

How is your preaching measuring up to that of Peter?

Additional insights: Note Peter's use of the four Names of God which are progressively mentioned (God/*Elohim,* Jesus/*Yahweh,* the Holy One/*HaKadosh,* and Lord/*Adonai*) as well as the Trinity within each section.

Four Types of Preaching

Preach the Word; be instant in season, out of season; reprove, rebuke, exhort with all longsuffering and doctrine.
  – 2 Timothy 4:2

In the New Testament, the word *preach* appears over 100 times translated from different Greek words to describe the preaching of Jesus and the Early Church. Analyzing the subtle differences between these words will aid the preacher in his preaching. Not all preaching is the same! According to William Barclay, there are four different types of preaching in the Early Church. (see William Barclay, *The Acts of the Apostles*, pp. 16-17)

Preaching is often characterized as an **EXCLAMATION**. This type of preaching is ***the persuasive statement of the essentials of the Gospel with the intent of evangelizing***. The

Greek words to describe this kind of preaching are *kerygma* (meaning to publish) and *euaggelizo* (meaning to bear witness). The emphasis of this type of preaching is the **heralding of the Gospel.**

Preaching is also characterized as an EXPLANATION. This type of preaching is *the giving of the meaning and significance of truth.* The Greek words to describe this kind of preaching are *didaskó* (meaning to instruct methodically truth or doctrine) and *dialegomai* (meaning to dialogue, discuss, or debate). The emphasis of this type of preaching is the **teaching of Truth.**

Preaching is further characterized as an EXHORTATION. This type of preaching is *the strong entreaty, consolation, or challenge.* The Greek words to describe this kind of preaching are *parakleis* (meaning to motivate, encourage) and *kataggello* (meaning to tell thoroughly). The emphasis of this type of preaching is the **motivating of the congregation.**

Lastly, preaching is characterized as an EXAMINATION. This type of preaching is *the pastoral communication or a short lecture with a moral theme.* The Greek words to describe this kind of preaching are *homilia* (meaning to give a short oration or talk with topical application) and *laleo* (meaning to discourse, talk or tell stories). The emphasis of this type of preaching is the **personal application of the Truth.**

Since all four of these types of preaching are attributed to Jesus or the Early Church as found in the New Testament, we must acknowledge that preaching takes on different styles, personalities, and applications as the Holy Spirit would direct. We must therefore recognize differences and be accepting of how God is using us or others to convey truth for a specific occasion.

Jesus Began To Preach

From that time Jesus began to preach...   – Matthew 4:17

Jesus' preaching employed all four of the types of preaching described by William Barkley: *Heralding the Gospel* (Exclamation), *Teaching the Truth* (Explanation), *Motivating the Congregation* (Exhortation), and personally *Applying the Truth* (Examination).

Jesus sought to **herald the Gospel** by preaching that men ought to repent, be born again, and be saved (see Matthew 3:12; Matthew 4:17; Luke 15:1-32; Matthew 13:15). In this regard, Jesus ministered as a true evangelist.

Jesus took time to **teach the Truth of Scripture** through discourse and parables (see Matthew 24; His forty-two parables). Jesus ministered as a teacher in explaining the Truths of Scripture.

Jesus also sought to **motivate His listeners** through challenging insights (see Matthew 5-7; Matthew 25). Jesus ministered as an encourager through strong entreaty.

Finally, Jesus sought to **apply the Truth** through dialogue, followed by a monologue of pertinent applications, with the Twelve (see Mark 4:3-32; John 13-14; Matthew 23). Through short topical application and moral themes, Jesus ministered as a shepherd to His listeners by answering their questions and concerns.

As we consider these four approaches to preaching by Jesus, we should ask ourselves, am I a one-tune preacher? When I go to the pulpit, even with my Spirit-given motivational gift, do I vary the approach in order to reach my listeners effectively? Or, is my preaching the same-old, same-old with the listeners drifting off to sleep through familiarity?

We should ask ourselves, which of the above four approaches to preaching will best communicate God's Word to this particular audience at this particular time?

Variety In Preaching

> *The Spirit of the Lord GOD is upon me; because the LORD hath anointed me to preach good tidings unto the meek; He hath sent me to bind up the brokenhearted, to proclaim liberty to the captives, and the opening of the prison to them that are bound;* – Isaiah 61:1

Before we move on to applying the second step of the Biblical pattern of discipleship to our preaching, let me encourage you to consider variety in preaching once again. We have seen how Jesus adapted His preaching to His listeners: *Heralding the Gospel* (Exclamation), *Teaching the Truth* (Explanation), *Motivating the Congregation* (Exhortation), and personally *Applying the Truth* (Examination).

Now I want to analyze some of the great preachers of Church history and also of our time. For which of the above four approaches are these preachers best known? You may even want to place an "H" (herald), "T" (teaching), "S" (sermon), or "D" (dialogue) beside each name that best describes their preaching.

Charles Spurgeon   John Wesley
Billy Graham   D.L. Moody
John Calvin   Charles Swindoll
W.A. Criswell   Stephen Olford
Adrian Rogers   Max Lucado
John Phillips

Now, further, although these preachers were all successful in their ministries, were they limiting themselves (and the Lord) by utilizing only one approach for which they were known? In other words, did they sometimes lose their audience by being a "one-tune" type of preacher? Indeed, I surmise, some people are turned off by certain types of preaching. Others get bored and restless after months and months of the same old sermon approach. They can almost close their eyes and sleep through the sermon,...and some do! Perhaps, others just leave our church and join another church. Could this have been prevented? Yes!

Consider Isaiah 61:1 and how Jesus used this multi-purposed text as His opening public statement in Luke 4:18-19. Should we not expand our opportunities to meet the varied needs of our congregation by varying our approach to preaching?

Separation

embracing virtue

add to your faith, virtue – 2 Peter 1:5

CHAPTER 3

A Life-Message Interpreted by Separation

I have preached righteousness in the great congregation: lo, I have not refrained my lips, O LORD, Thou knowest.
— Psalm 40:9

As we continue to apply the Biblical steps of discipleship to our preaching, we move from faith to virtue, from salvation to separation. Clearly, preaching a life-message must be initiated by *salvation*! A message that will transform another person's life is a message that is built in the preacher's life! However, interpreting that life-message of faith through *personal virtue* is just as vital.

Many world religions emphasize piety or holiness as a means to an end. In Christianity, on the other hand, holiness grows out of a relationship with the God of grace! Believers do not work their way up the spiritual ladder to God. Instead, God has come down to their level through the incarnation of Jesus. Conversion, to the Apostle Paul, was *putting off the old man and putting on the new man.* (See Ephesians 4:20-25.)

When Jesus stated in Matthew 5:20, that *except your righteousness exceed the righteousness of the scribes and Pharisees*, He was not encouraging His followers to replace Jewish legalism with Christian legalism! He was correcting abusive leadership within Judaism. The Pharisees preached one message but lived another. For them it was do-as-I-say, not-do-as-I-do! Such hypocrisy was not to be so with the followers of Jesus!

The disciples of Jesus, particularly those who preach the Word, are to build a life-message that is consistent with their walk. We are to be **separate in our behavior** as well as **sound in our beliefs**! If we are going to preach with conviction and power, we must excel in a life of separation!

Understanding a Life of Separation

Wherefore come out from among them, and be ye separate.
– 2 Corinthians 6:17

From the call of Abraham in Genesis 12:1 (*Now the LORD had said unto Abram, Get thee out of thy country, and from thy kindred, and from thy father's house, unto a land that I will shew thee*), to the Sermon on the Mount in Matthew 5:20 (*That except your righteousness shall exceed the righteousness of the scribes and Pharisees,...*), the Scriptures have been clear that we are to be holy even as God is holy! (See Exodus 19:6; Leviticus 11:45; Luke 1:74-75; Hebrews 12:14; 1 Peter 1:15-16.)

In order to live a separated life, one must understand his enemies: the flesh, the world, and the devil! The inter-workings of these three enemies form strongholds like a multi-turreted medieval castle. Only the weapons of our warfare can bring down these strongholds. (See Ephesians 6:11-18; 2 Corinthians 10:4.) In the life of the preacher, they must come down! What does not come down will subtly be raised up within the life of his listeners!

Finding victory over stronghold-sins that have been formed within the life of the preacher means that victory will need to be achieved in more than one area of the preacher's life! This is non-negotiable! Victory here means victory in the lives of others!

> *But ye are a chosen generation, a royal priesthood, a holy nation, a peculiar people; that ye should show forth the praises of Him Who hath called you out of darkness into His marvelous light. – 1 Peter 2:9*

Same Ol' Same Ol'

> *And seeing the multitudes, He went up into a mountain: and when He was set, His disciples came unto Him, And He opened His mouth, and taught them, saying,...*
> – Matthew 5:1-2

When the multitudes came to Jesus, He departed to a mountain and waited for His newly-called disciples to come to Him. After their arrival, Jesus began to teach His disciples the essential principles of discipleship in what is often referred to as the Sermon on the Mount. In His teaching, He addressed familiar arguments that were dividing Judaism between the teachings of Rabbi Hillel and Rabbi Gamilael. They were the same old arguments debated over and over again, hundreds of times!

Jesus exposed the root of the problem: morality was dictating theology! The moral bias was like a broken compass. It pointed in the direction that the person wanted it to point! For the Pharisees, this was a tricky debate tactic of "widening and narrowing" the discussion. They would find an extreme example and then use it to justify their wrongdoing! Sound familiar?

Jesus wasn't fooled by their bias or their tactic! He responded with six quick, but controversial topics. Follow Jesus' reasoning in each of these areas as seen in Matthew 5.

- ☐ ***Murder***: The Pharisees narrowed the definition of murder. Jesus widened it to include hate! – v 21-26
- ☐ ***Adultery***: The Pharisees narrowed the definition of adultery. Jesus widened it to include lust! – v 27-30
- ☐ ***Divorce***: The Pharisees widened the definition of divorce. Jesus narrowed it to include adultery! – v 31-32
- ☐ ***Oaths***: The Pharisees narrowed the definition of oaths. Jesus widened it to include honesty! – v 33-37
- ☐ ***Revenge***: The Pharisees widened the definition of revenge. Jesus narrowed it to include non-violence! – v 38-42
- ☐ ***Enemies***: The Pharisees narrowed the definition of enemies. Jesus widened it to include neighbors! – v 43-48

We are not called to win debates. We are called to live a separated lifestyle through a clear conscience. Thus, we should be careful that we are not seeking to justify our moral bias!

> *Woe unto them that call evil good, and good evil; that put darkness for light, and light for darkness; that put bitter for sweet, and sweet for bitter! Woe unto them that are wise in their own eyes, and prudent in their own sight!*
> – Isaiah 5:20-21

Principles of Separation

> *Wherefore come out from among them, and be ye separate, saith the Lord, and touch not the unclean thing; and I will receive you.* – 2 Corinthians 6:17

Continuing our theme of a life-message interpreted by separation, we come to an important distinction for the preacher, namely, living and preaching by principles instead of by legalism. We do not deny that there are clear prohibitions in both the Old and New Testaments, but many issues are not directly addressed. Hence, the preacher needs to have some guiding ethical principles that govern his life. Paul wrote his first epistle to the Corinthians with this goal in mind.

The Principle of Evidence – (1 Corinthians 6:11) Paul began his discussion concerning governing principles for a lifestyle of separation in 1 Corinthians by describing the believer: *And such were some of you: but ye are washed, but ye are sanctified, but ye are justified in the name of the Lord Jesus, and by the Spirit of our God.* Paul declared that the believer is washed, sanctified, and justified! Living a separated life from our old life of sin gives true evidence of our salvation! We are to put off the old man and put on a new man! So ask yourself, how does this activity reflect upon my new nature as a Christian? Will continuing in this activity draw into question my conversion experience? Will this activity give further credence to my testimony of salvation?

The Principle of Expediency – (1 Corinthians 6:12a) Paul declared that *All things are lawful for me, but all things are not helpful.* It is so easy for the pastor to fail to establish and be faithful to his priorities! He must discipline himself to ask concerning any expenditure of his time: Does this activity hinder my accomplishing my life's goals and God's purposes in my life? What specifically does God's Word state about this activity? Will I surrender to God's expressed truths in this area?

The Principle of Enslavement – (1 Corinthians 6:12b) Paul declared that he would not be brought under the power of any legalism: *All things are lawful for me, but I will not be brought under the power of any.* Through Christ, we have tremendous freedoms, but not if these freedoms lead us to compromise our convictions. So ask yourself, does this activity have any power over my body, mind, emotions, or schedule? Will this activity have an addictive influence upon my life? Will this enslavement impact my ministry and preaching?

The Principle of Embodiment – (1 Corinthians 6:19) Paul posed a deeply challenging question: *What? Know ye not that your body is the temple of the Holy Ghost Which is in you, Which ye have in God and ye are not your own?* The preacher must acknowledge that the Holy Spirit resides within him! So, ask yourself, is there a possibility that I will allow this activity to control my life? Will this activity grieve the Holy Spirit? Am I genuinely Spirit-controlled as I face this temptation?

The Principle of Example – (1 Corinthians 8:9) A couple of chapters later, Paul continued his challenge concerning a separated lifestyle by warning: *But beware lest somehow this liberty of yours become a stumbling block to those who are weak.* Every believer, but especially the preacher, must choose his activities with a sensitivity to others. He must be willing to sacrifice his own selfish satisfaction for the sake of others. Proverbs 18:19 warns: *A brother offended is harder to be won than a strong city: and their contentions are like the bars of a castle.* The preacher must ask: will my involvement in this activity cause someone else to stumble or at least justify a violation of a conviction? Would I have to compromise my leadership position within the Body of Christ in order to participate in this activity? Will my suffering while resisting the temptation enhance my example before weaker brothers?

The Principle of Edification – (1 Corinthians 10:23) Again, Paul emphasized the importance of the benefit of an activity to God's purposes, but he carried the concept further by focusing on the personal benefit that comes from an activity: *All things are lawful for me, but all things are not helpful; all things are lawful for me, but all things do not edify.* Ask yourself, will this activity refresh me mentally, physically, morally, emotionally, or spiritually or will it drain me in any of these areas? In considering this activity, am I being sensitive to the needs of others within my sphere of influence?

The Principle of Exaltation – (1 Corinthians 10:31) Paul clearly stated the priority principle that should govern our lifestyle: *Therefore, whether you eat or drink, or whatever you do, do all to the glory of God.* Will this activity allow me the freedom to acknowledge Christ through my participation? In what specific ways will God be glorified through my involvement in this activity?

The Principle of Evangelism – (1 Corinthians 10:32-33) It is no surprise that a man driven by evangelism would establish that end as a governing principle in his activities: *Give no offense, either to the Jews or to the Greeks or to the church of God, just as I also please all men in all things, not seeking my own profit, but the profit of many, that they may be saved.* Ask yourself: will this activity limit or increase my evangelistic opportunities? If my lost family and friends discovered my involvement in this activity, would my witness be enhanced or nullified?

Living by principles avoids the legalism-trap of having to abide by rules and seeking to find new exceptions or loopholes. The Old Testament Law taught us that we will never measure up to God's standards. However, living by principles allows us the flexibility to live the Christ-life in various situations. Allow me to encourage you to post this list of Paul's principles for a separated lifestyle in a place with quick access for regular examination:

- ☐ **Evidence** (Will this activity or choice give question to my new life in Christ?)
- ☐ **Enslavement** (Will this activity or choice return me to bondage to sin?)
- ☐ **Expediency** (Will this activity or choice obstruct my purpose to live according to God's Word?)
- ☐ **Embodiment** (Will this activity or choice bring grief to the Holy Spirit Who now dwells in my body?)
- ☐ **Example** (Will this activity or choice cause weaker believers to justify their sinful lifestyle?)
- ☐ **Edification** (Will this activity or choice build up those who are around me?)

As they ministered to the Lord, and fasted, the Holy Ghost said, Separate Me Barnabas and Saul for the work whereunto I have called them. – Acts 13:2

Surrender

embracing knowledge

And to virtue, knowledge – 2 Peter 1:5

CHAPTER 4

A Life-Message Integrated by Surrender

And moreover, because the preacher was wise, he still taught the people knowledge; yea, he gave good heed, and sought out, and set in order many proverbs. – Ecclesiastes 12:9

Thus far, we have considered two essential principles in applying the Biblical steps of discipleship to our preaching. The first principle is **a life-message initiated by salvation**. Through a personal relationship with God's Son, Jesus, the preacher can and should preach with boldness! Personally knowing Jesus is the first step of faith and a vital step that cannot be skipped. Yet there are many preachers scattered across the globe who do not have a personal relationship with Jesus!

The second principle that should impact our preaching is **a life-message interpreted by separation**. With a lifestyle of being separated from the flesh and the world, the preacher can preach with the confidence that Christ's message does indeed change people! If this step is skipped, disaster will sooner or later follow! Compromise with sin weakens the preacher's ability to reach his congregation!

As we continue to explore how to apply the Biblical steps of discipleship to our preaching, we now consider **a life-message integrated through surrender**. To be effective and faithful, the preacher must preach the inerrant, infallible, and inspired Word of God. To do so, he must first surrender to those truths he is going to preach! Many preachers have head knowledge of truth, perhaps even conservative viewpoints, but have not fully surrendered to the truths contained in the Scriptures!

In surrendering and obeying the Word of God, the preacher must develop a **Biblical worldview**. A Biblical worldview is distinctively different from a **Christian worldview** that merely takes conservative positions on moral issues. A Biblical worldview is far more inclusive. The Scriptures should form our only basis for faith and practice, and the preacher must be disciplined to internalize the whole body of Truth.

> *Study to show thyself approved unto God, a workman that needeth not to be ashamed rightly dividing the Word of truth.* — 2 Timothy 2:15

My Gospel

> *Now to Him that is of power to establish you according to my gospel, and the preaching of Jesus Christ, according to the revelation of the mystery, which was kept secret since the world began.* — Romans 16:25

Thirteen times in the book of Romans alone, Paul refers to the gospel. He describes it as *the gospel of Christ, the gospel of peace,* and *the gospel of God*. But his phrase that has always caught my attention is ***my gospel***.

Joseph Carrol has succinctly stated, "Truth does not become mine until it becomes me!" In other words, for the preacher, the gospel is not an academic or theological issue. The gospel must take full possession of the preacher! He must surrender to it!

By the "gospel," Paul was referring to that template — that frame of reference or that pattern — that had been given to him through the preaching of Jesus Christ. We might call it today a Biblical worldview. In the early verses of his epistle, Paul wrote that he was anxious to preach this Biblical worldview to the Romans (Romans 1:15). In his presentation of this Biblical worldview, Paul divided the gospel into two major thoughts: The Analysis of a Biblical Worldview (Romans 1-11), and The Application of a Biblical Worldview (Romans 12-16).

It seems Paul's entire purpose in writing the book of Romans was to present an analysis and application of a Biblical worldview. In the early chapters of the book, he uniquely defined God, sin, salvation, and Judaism. Then in the later chapters of the book, Paul presented the application of his Biblical worldview by describing how the gospel should impact the local church, the government, business practices, and personal relationships.

Concluding questions: What is your "gospel"? When you say that you preach the "gospel," does it line up with the Biblical worldview that Paul presented as his gospel in the book of Romans? Are you truly surrendered to the truth of Paul's gospel?

> *And they, when they had testified and preached the words of the Lord, returned to Jerusalem and preached the gospel in many villages of the Samaritans.* – Acts 8:25

Rightly Dividing the Word of Truth

> *Study to show thyself approved unto God, a workman that needeth not to be ashamed rightly dividing the word of truth.*
> – 2 Timothy 2:15

One of the greatest failures of today's educational system is not teaching good study habits. One of the greatest needs among preachers is forming good study habits when dealing with the Word of God. If we are commissioned to preach, then we are charged with studying. Here, there are no shortcuts! Our disciplines, or the lack thereof, will become apparent to our listeners. There are at least twelve tools needed to comprehend the Scriptures properly. A true student of the Word must become thoroughly familiar with and disciplined to employ each of these tools.

- ☐ The **Geography** of the lands of the Bible, particularly the Holy Land
- ☐ The **Cultures** of the nations and the people
- ☐ The **Mysteries** described in the Scriptures
- ☐ The **Names** of God and key Bible personages
- ☐ The **Symbols** mentioned throughout the Word
- ☐ The **Covenants** that God made with the People of God
- ☐ The **Prophecies** and their principles of understanding
- ☐ The **Numbers** mentioned throughout the Word and their meanings
- ☐ The **Figures of speech** and the context of each text used in preaching
- ☐ The **Principles** of interpretation that unlock the understanding behind the word meanings
- ☐ The **Distinctions** within the Word as God that divide people groups, judgments, etc.
- ☐ The **Survey** of the Scriptures demonstrates the relationship of different books of the Bible with each other.

With these tools, the preacher will be able to divide and discern a section of Scripture quickly. Then he will be able to stand before his listeners and say, Thus saith the Lord!

The Lord GOD hath given me the tongue of the learned, that I should know how to speak a word in season to him that is weary: He wakeneth morning by morning, He wakeneth mine ear to hear as the learned.   – Isaiah 50:4

Correctly Dissecting the Word of Truth

Study to show thyself approved unto God, a workman that needeth not to be ashamed rightly dividing the word of truth.
       – 2 Timothy 2:15

Preachers are surgeons who are able to dissect the Scriptures correctly! In 2 Timothy 2:15, the Apostle Paul used a compound word that means *to make a straight cut*. A preacher is like a medical surgeon who has studied the patient's disease and now sets forth to make the precise incision that will expose the disease and allow the surgeon to extract it. The preacher, as he prayerfully severs the Word of God, allows the Spirit to extract the spiritual disease!

My mentor, the late Dr. Stephen Olford, used to train us to look at any given passage and make the correct incision. He stressed that we should look for the **dominating theme**, the **integrating thoughts**, and the **motivating thrust**.

First, the preacher should examine the text in its context and ask the Holy Spirit to guide him to discover the dominating theme of the passage. From the broader context of each book down to the more concise context of the passage, he should seek to discover the primary subject matter. **The preacher must ask what theme is expressed by the writer in the given passage.**

Second, the preacher should look for the integrating thoughts that serve as the skeleton and the sinews of the passage. God is a God of order as so acutely observed in nature. His Word has structure! After discovering the skeleton and the sinews of the passage, the cut can be made precisely! **The preacher must ask what integrating thoughts help explain the author's intent.**

Lastly, the preacher should look for the motivating thrust that God intended. Each passage of Scripture had and still has a specific purpose. With each word — indeed, with each stroke of each letter — the Holy Spirit is guiding the reader to the heart of the matter. **The preacher must ask what the conclusion of the matter is. Why did the Spirit guide the author to write this passage?**

The task of the preacher is to discover the correct dissection of the passage. And then, with equal skill, he is to open up the Scripture to the listener in such a way that the hearer will, by faith, understand that passage. Surely this is a daunting task! Imagine the preacher standing before a congregation with a scalpel in his hand poised to make that straight cut! With confidence, he then must be able to boldly say, as Jesus did, *Let these sayings sink down into your ears!* (Luke 9:44). With that, the cut is made, and the spiritual surgery begins!

> *For the word of God is quick, and powerful, and sharper than any two edged sword, piercing even to the dividing asunder of soul and spirit, and of the joints and marrow, and is a discerner of the thoughts and intents of the heart.*
> *– Hebrews 4:12*

Wholeness of Scripture

> *And He said unto them, These are the words which I spake unto you, while I was yet with you, that all things must be fulfilled, which were written in the law of Moses, and in the prophets, and in the psalms, concerning Me.* – Luke 24:44

I was challenged as a fourteen-year-old boy to read the Bible from Genesis to Revelation when I heard a friend comment that most Christians have never read the entire Bible. So I made for myself a project of reading the Bible from start to finish during the month of June. I used my oldest brother's King James Version of the Bible. The power of the words I read brought me to the conviction of my personal sin. When I reached the end of the month, I repented of my sins, asked Jesus to forgive me, and gave my life to Him to be my Lord and Savior.

A few weeks later, I picked up another Bible. That, too, was a life-changing experience! As I glanced through the Bible, I noticed various Scripture cross-references down the middle margin of the page. The earlier Bible did not have a column of cross-references. I was curious and began looking up the various verses. In fact, I spent the entire day looking up related references. This was one of the most rewarding days of my life! As I continued to look up references from throughout the Bible, something miraculous happened that has greatly impacted my life – and should impact the life of everyone who preaches the Word. The Bible became one unit! Not sixty-six individual books, but one inspired and inerrant book! I saw a supernatural unity. That experience has never lost its impact!

When Jesus spoke to the disciples in one of His resurrection appearances, He referred to the Pentateuch of Moses, the wisdom section, including the Psalms, and the Prophets. He brought wholeness to the Scriptures! He was saying to the disciples that God's Word was one inspired and unified book! Jesus never questioned the Scriptures as being anything but equal in inspiration. From Genesis all the way through Malachi, the Word is inspired! From Matthew through Revelation, the Word is equally inspired! There is not a hint of a two-tiered Bible, where one part is more inspired than another.

The discovery of the wholeness of Scripture produced a complete confidence in God's inspired Word! That confidence has throughout my years impacted my devotional times, my walk with the Lord, my counseling of others, and my many pulpit opportunities! May I encourage you to ask God to give you a fresh vision of the complete, inspired Bible!

> *All Scripture is given by inspiration of God, and is profitable for doctrine, for reproof, for correction, for instruction in righteousness.* – 2 Timothy 3:16

Nothing Beyond What Is Written

> *In writing this much, brethren, with special reference to Apollos and myself, I have done so for your sakes, in order to teach you by example what those words mean, which say, Nothing beyond what is written.* – 1 Corinthians 4:6 (Weymouth)

For those of us who are committed to the inspired, inerrant, and infallible Word of God, Paul recorded a well-known saying among the early Christians: *nothing beyond what is written*! The apostle was declaring that the Word of God is our final authority on all matters – our only rule of faith and practice! In one profound verse, Paul sweeps away, for all time, any possible contenders!

Paul rejected the **Folly of Human Reason** as a possible final authority! When Satan tempted Jesus, Jesus refused to rely on reasoning. His response was to quote the Word of God. Throughout His ministry, Jesus often asked the question, "Have you not read?" Today, we too must dismiss the folly of human reasoning, whether it's evolution, education, politics, medicine, or even the institutional church. What matters is the revelation of God, as found in the Word of God.

Paul further rejected the **Folly of Special Revelation** as a possible final authority! Many religious groups weigh in with their spin of special revelation. It may come from the church councils with their often contradictory and confusing conclusions. Or it could come from well crafted creeds and statements of faith that are often put on the same par as the Word of God. Perhaps it comes from various books and articles. Sometimes, a special revelation is found in local church by-laws and constitutions that form denominational litmus tests. Other places where special revelation shows up are from visions, dreams, and words of knowledge by self-proclaimed prophets or from the many conference and television speakers that hold a pied-piper spell over their many listeners. But Paul declared that the only source of authority should be the written Word of God.

Paul also rejected the **Folly of Personal Rationality** as a possible final authority! Just as the Pharisees widened or narrowed their moral definitions and interpretations of the Law to suit their lifestyle, today, some rationalize improper lifestyles such as divorce and remarriage, abortion, pornography, addictions, adultery, homosexuality, and Satanic style music. Their rationality becomes their trap. Only the authority in the written Word of God gives freedom.

Lastly, Paul rejected the **Folly of Man-made Religions** as a possible final authority! From the beginning, the world has been filled with a parade of religions seeking to convince the naive that theirs is the real revelation. These false religions and cults blatantly contradict the written Word of God. They are not part of the historical, true Revelation of our God.

The Apostle Paul provided us with discernment and confidence with one simple and yet comprehensive statement: *nothing beyond what is written!*

All Scripture is given by inspiration of God,...
– 2 Timothy 3:16a

Preach the Word

How sweet are Thy words unto my taste! Yea, sweeter than honey to my mouth! – Psalm 119:103

During my college days, I was told by my mother that the nearby Methodist Church was having a revival. I was somewhat familiar with the great Methodist revivalists of church history, so I went one evening to hear the itinerant revivalist. As he preached, he stated, "I don't see how John Wesley ever got so many converts by filling his sermon with so many dry Scriptures!" I was taken back! "Dried Scriptures?" I thought! "Well, that is exactly how he did it!" And what about this upstart of a revivalist? He used one verse in passing, and only one person responded to his message!

The Apostle Paul admonished his readers in Romans 10:8: *But what saith it? The word is nigh thee even in thy mouth, and in thy heart: that is, the word of faith, which we preach.* In other words, Paul set the example for the rest of Christian preachers to follow. His formula was simple: just preach the Word of God!

Decades later, after hearing that Methodist speaker, I heard a Baptist preacher of some note read from John Bunyan's *Pilgrim's Progress*...as his sermon text! From there, he expounded several readings from Bunyan's book as his sermon! I remember asking myself, which of these two preachers – the Methodist revivalist or the Baptist preacher – was worse? The one who mocked at Scripture or the one who substituted man's words for God's Word? Essentially, they are of the same stripe!

Preacher, my counsel to you is to preach the Word – boldly and unapologetically! And, preferably, expositorily.

Preach the word; be instant in season, out of season; reprove, rebuke, exhort with all longsuffering and doctrine.
— 2 Timothy 4:2

God's Trinity of Truths

In the beginning God created the heaven and the earth. And the earth was without form, and void; and darkness was upon the face of the deep. And the Spirit of God moved upon the face of the waters. And God said, Let there be light: and there was light. — Genesis 1:1-3

As previously stated, God begins the Book of Genesis with a self revelation of His triune nature. This concept of the trinity is, I believe, the key that unlocks many doctrinal debates. Often I hear believers debating over some doctrinal teaching that they hold dear. Each side appeals to Bible verses that support his view. The result is that sincere people have become divided into opposing camps with each feeling that their position is the only correct one. I surmise that the balance of truth is found in a third position, forming what I call "God's Trinity of Truths".

Listed below are a few truths that demonstrate the trinity of many doctrines:

- **Godhead** – God the Father, God the Son, and God the Holy Spirit (2 Corinthians 13:14)
- **Prominent Names of God** – Elohim, Adonai, and Jehovah (Isaiah 43:3, 10-11)
- **Nature of Jesus** – divinity, humanity, and personality (Philippians 2:5-11)

- ☐ **Word of God** – divine inspiration, human authorship, and personal penmanship (2 Peter 1:21)
- ☐ **Revelation of Truth** – general revelation, special revelation, and personal revelation or insights (John 1:1-5)
- ☐ **Nature of Man** – body, soul, and spirit (1 Thessalonians 5:23)
- ☐ **Problem with Man** – sin, iniquity, and transgression (Exodus 34:7)
- ☐ **Sin** – lust, greed, and pride (1 John 2:16)
- ☐ **Salvation** – grace of God, will of man, and faith of believer (Ephesians 2:8-10)
- ☐ **Christian Life** – faith, hope, and love (1 Corinthians 13:13)
- ☐ **Disciplines** – outward giving, upward prayer, and inward self-denial (Matthew 6:1-21)
- ☐ **Judgments** – uncleanness, vile affections, and reprobate mind (Romans 1:1-32)
- ☐ **Governments** – Israel, Gentiles, and Church (1 Corinthians 10:32)

As the preacher surrenders to the Truth of God's Word, he will benefit by applying the often-repeated anonymous quote: "In all things essential, unity; In all things secondary, liberty; and In all things, charity!"

Endeavoring to keep the unity of the Spirit in the bond of peace. — Ephesians 4:3

Spirit-Control

embracing temperance

And to knowledge, temperance – 2 Peter 1:6a

CHAPTER 5

A Life-Message Inspired by Spirit-Control

But if the Spirit of Him that raised up Jesus from the dead dwell in you, He that raised up Christ from the dead shall also quicken your mortal bodies by His Spirit that dwelleth in you... Likewise the Spirit also helpeth our infirmities:
— Romans 8:11, 26a

As the believer develops **a life-message integrated through surrender** to the Truths of God's Word, he quickly recognizes that his own self-discipline is not sufficient to attain the goal. He requires **a life-message inspired by Spirit-control**! Our culture is full of self-help programs that focus on forgiveness, humility, self-denial, and self-regulation, but these valuable tools can only yield consistent temperance through the supernatural, quickening inspiration of the Holy Spirit. Both in the New Testament listings of Jesus' and the disciples' steps of discipleship and in God's directions for Israel's annual curriculum of feasts, the Holy Spirit's role in making disciples is right in the center! It is only His control that makes the Biblical steps of discipleship effective. His breathing life into both our personal walk and our preaching must be central!

Not by might nor by power, but by My Spirit says the Lord Almighty   — Zachariah 4:6

The Spirit's Anointing in Preaching

The Spirit of the Lord is upon Me, because He hath anointed Me to preach the gospel....   – Luke 4:18a

At Nazareth, Jesus stood and read from Isaiah 61:1: *The Spirit of the Lord GOD is upon me; because the LORD hath anointed me to preach good tidings unto the meek....* Here marked the beginning of Jesus' ministry and His opening statement set the principle for the preaching that His listeners would come to expect – anointed preaching.

I well remember counseling a pastor in southern Michigan concerning the work of the Holy Spirit during preaching. Sadly he responded by saying, "I have never heard of such a thing as anointed preaching!" For the Christian pastor, there should be no other kind of preaching!

The Scriptures are clear repeatedly concerning the work of the Holy Spirit in the believer.

First, there is the **incoming** of the Holy Spirit at the time of conversion. This is the **adoptive** work of the Spirit (John 3:5; Acts 5:32; 1 Corinthians 12:13). The Holy Spirit takes up residence in the life and body of the believer.

Second, there is the **indwelling** of the Holy Spirit throughout the lifetime of the believer. This is the **abiding** work of the Spirit (Galatians 3:14; 1 Corinthians 3:16). Jesus taught that the Spirit is given to His followers and that He would abide with them forever (John 14:16).

Third, there is the **infilling** of the Holy Spirit at the time of significant service. This is the **administrative** work of the Spirit (Luke 11:13; Ephesians 5:18). Christians are well equipped for ministry through the workings of the Spirit within the believer.

Fourth, there is also the **inshining** of the Holy Spirit through the preaching of the Word of God. This is the

anointing work of the Spirit (Matthew 5:16; John 5:33; Acts 2:4; Acts 4:31). When the pastor preaches, the congregation should be hearing two voices: the voice of the pastor and, more importantly, the voice of the Spirit of God!

Let me be crystal clear at this point, the anointing of the Spirit is a special work in which the Word of God takes on a dynamic that brings conviction and conversion to the listeners! This anointing is indispensable!

So then faith cometh by hearing, and hearing by the word of God. – Romans 10:17

Preparing to Preach

But my horn shalt Thou exalt like the horn of an unicorn: I shall be anointed with fresh oil. – Psalm 92:10

While Scripture confirms that the Word of the Lord comes from God, it also challenges the preacher to be diligent in *the preparations of the heart.* (See Proverbs 16:1.) There is no substitute for personal preparation before going to God's people with the message from God! Knowing that a message prepared merely in the mind reaches only a mind, but a message prepared in the heart reaches a heart, the preacher must place a great priority on his time and efforts in getting the message of God into his heart before addressing God's people.

For many years, Psalm 92:10 (above) has been my prayer tool to examine my heart before preaching. In this verse, the aged King David sought God's fresh anointing! Six individuals were anointed in the Scriptures. Utilizing each of these anointings, I bring myself before the Lord before I preach.

The **LEPERS** were anointed following their being cleansed of leprosy, a sign of sin (Leviticus 14:18). They were anointed as **a sign of cleansing**. I ask myself, is my confession of the Biblical sin lists up to date? (See Mark 7:20-23; Colossians 3:5,8,9; Galatians 5:19-21; 1 Corinthians 6:9-10; and Revelation 21:8.) Am I clean before God?

The **KINGS** were anointed for leadership (1 Samuel 16:13). Those who would exercise leadership in God's stead were anointed. They would be anointed as **a sign of authority**. As I stand before the people, I ask God to help me recognize the awesome responsibility of standing in His place. I acknowledge that I must depend solely upon Him. I ask that my sermon would reflect spiritual authority as the Spirit flows through me.

The **PRIESTS** were anointed for their representation of the people before God (Exodus 28:41). As intercessors, they brought the people before God. They would be anointed as **a sign of the people's representative**. As I prepare to minister the Word, I seek to realize that I am, in reality, taking the people's hurts and pains before the Lord.

The **PROPHETS** were anointed for their representation of God before the people (1 Chronicles 16:22). They were God's spokesmen. They were anointed as **a sign of God's representative**. I ask the Lord for boldness to preach His Word and freedom from any compromise. I pray that all that comes out of my mouth will be the purity of His Word and free from all that is false.

The **BONDSERVANTS** were anointed for their commitment to serve (Joel 2:29). Their anointing was **a sign of obedient servanthood**. Jesus taught that we should not strive to lord over others, but instead be the bondservant to all. I examine myself for humility toward my congregation and my peers. At the same time, I pray that the Lord will help me to keep my priority to serve Him higher than my priority to serve the people. I ask for deliverance from all drive to please the people in my message. I examine my personal obedience to all that God has required.

The **SICK** were anointed to honor God in their healing (Mark 6:13). Often priests or elders would anoint with oil those who were ill in order to initiate healing as well. The anointing of the sick was **a sign of physical neediness**. Whether it was a need to quell butterflies during my early preaching years or to relieve infirmities in my elderly years, I find the Lord faithful to overcome my physical neediness as I seek Him for healing before preaching!

Before you preach, BE PREPARED!

And your feet shod with the preparation of the gospel of peace. – Ephesians 6:15

Basic Understanding of Spiritual Gifts

Now concerning spiritual gifts, brethren, I would not have you ignorant. – 1 Corinthians 12:1

Under the leadership of the Holy Spirit, the Apostle Paul desired his readers to understand spiritual gifts in order to utilize them in preaching and serving. To accomplish his desire requires a deep, but basic understanding of the text found in 1 Corinthians 12:4-6.

First, in verse four, Paul wrote that there are **motivations** (*charismaton*) of the Spirit. Motivations are the basic **spiritual inward drive** given by God the Spirit in order to minister. These gifts are listed and expanded in Romans 12:6-8. Specifically, they are prophesy, serving, teaching, exhorting, giving, ruling, and showing mercy. The Holy Spirit permanently gives each believer one of these motivating gifts with which he is to minister. This gift is not sought by the believer since it is selected and chosen by the Spirit.

Second, in verse five, Paul wrote that there are **ministries** (*diakonion*) of the Spirit. Ministries are the **special opportunities of service** as given by God the Son. These opportunities of service are enumerated in 1 Corinthians 12:27-31 and Ephesians 4:11-12. Specifically, they are apostle (or missionary), prophet (or revivalist), evangelist, pastor, teacher, worker of power, worker of healings, helper, administrator, and linguist. Through the use of the believer's motivating gift, God will open up varying opportunities for service. These opportunities may change often throughout the believer's lifetime of service.

Third, in verse six, Paul wrote that there are **manifestations** (*energman phanerosis*) of God. Manifestations are the **actual results** in the lives of others as directed from God the Father. The results are listed in 1 Corinthians 12:7-11. Specifically, they include word of wisdom, knowledge, faith, healings, miracles, word of prophecy, distinguishing spirits, interpreting of languages, and translating of languages. Through the use of the believer's motivating gift, he will serve in varying opportunities with different results in the lives of those to whom he serves. These impacts can vary widely in different people, even at the same opportunity of service.

As the Holy Spirit directs, each of us should strive to work together – using our motivating gift through many ministry opportunities opened to us and, then, leave the resulting manifestations up to God. In this way, the Body of Christ functions effortlessly but effectively, and God receives all the glory!

For we are laborers together with God. – 1 Corinthians 3:6

Hindering the Work of the Holy Spirit

They kept not the covenant of God, and refused to walk in His law.   – Psalm 78:10

How very grievous it is for a congregation to limit the labor of a pastor by not keeping God's covenant and refusing to walk in His law! So it was with the nation of Israel when the Holy Spirit used Asaph to describe in Psalm 78 the activity of hindering His work. In this all-encompassing chapter, the law of full mention is employed as the five-fold degeneration of sin against the Holy Spirit is described in complete detail in a single location. Asaph skillfully utilized the ever-worsening relationship of Israel with the Lord during their wilderness journey.

Asaph began his Psalm (verses 1-8) with the wonderful purpose that God had for His people: that they would live in such a way that future generations would embrace the way of living that had been given to them by their fathers. It was God's purpose for them to praise Him and to place their hope in Him. Yet, the Israelites became a stubborn and rebellious generation that did not set their hearts aright. The remainder of Asaph's Psalm is a sad commentary concerning the Israelites, but also, an instructive commentary for today's congregations.

First, Asaph described Israel's **Resisting Sin** against the Holy Spirit (verses 9-17). The Israelites did not keep the covenant, they refused to walk in God's law, and they forgot God's works and wonders! God did marvelous works in their midst, but they withstood the Lord again and again. This type of disobedience is referred to in Acts 7:51 as **resisting** the Holy Spirit.

Second, Asaph described Israel's **Restraining Sin** against the Holy Spirit (verses18-33). The Israelites did not stop at merely resisting the Holy Spirit. They spoke against the Lord and refused to believe God and His plan of salvation. In response, God brought remedial judgment upon them. In Acts 5:9, the New Testament refers to this limiting action as **tempting** the Holy Spirit.

Third, Asaph described Israel's **Repressing Sin** against the Holy Spirit (verses 34-37). The Israelites responded to God's remedial judgment with unbridled lust and further deepened their sin! In Acts 5:3-4, the New Testament refers to this type of degenerative action as **lying** to the Holy Spirit!

Fourth, Asaph described Israel's **Refusing Sin** against the Holy Spirit (verses 38-40). Out of God's compassion, He allowed Israel time to respond properly, yet they provoked Him even further. In Ephesians 4:30, Paul refers to this type of continued disobedience as **grieving** the Holy Spirit.

Finally, Asaph described Israel's **Rejecting Sin** against the Holy Spirit (verses 41-64). Eventually, the Israelites took a fatal step by provoking the Holy Spirit to anger as they embraced graven images! God responded quickly by forsaking the Tabernacle and delivering the Israelites into the enemy's hands. All but two died in the wilderness, cut off from the Promise Land! In 1 Thessalonians 5:19, Paul speaks of this type of ultimate rejection as **quenching** the Holy Spirit.

What a sad commentary Asaph presents before us! Yet worse than sad is what takes place in many congregations where individuals, despite this warning example in Psalm 78, follow the same downward path: resisting, restraining, repressing, refusing, and finally rejecting the Holy Spirit. The pastor of such a congregation can gain discernment from Asaph's presentation, but he can also gain encouragement, for Asaph did not stop with verse 64. He closed his Psalm with the reminder that God had a remnant in Judah (verses 65-72). God always preserves a remnant who will still do His work with integrity! Find those remnant believers and "go with the goers"!

> *So He fed them according to the integrity of His heart; and guided them by the skillfulness of His hands.* – Psalm 78:72

Our Reluctant God

> *And the LORD said, My Spirit shall not always strive with man, for that he also is flesh: yet his days shall be an hundred and twenty years.* – Genesis 6:3

As we continue our focus on the work of the Spirit in the life and preaching of the minister, a three-letter word in Genesis 6:3 cannot be overlooked: that little word "yet"! The Holy Spirit was first introduced to Man in Genesis 1:2: *And the earth was without form, and void; and darkness was upon the face of the deep. And the Spirit of God moved upon the face of the waters.* What a powerful testimony of the Spirit energizing and creating the universe! At the same time, this verse prophetically speaks to the condition of Man in his fallen state – lifeless, empty, and unenlightened spiritually! Only the quickening and recreating work of the Holy Spirit can bring life!

The second reference to the Holy Spirit in Scripture is found in our text in Genesis 6:3. Many a preacher has come down hard on the warning that the Spirit of God has a threshold of patience. When Man's sin goes beyond God's patience, then consequences for his actions take place. Most preachers, however, miss that little word in the text: yet! God's Spirit did bring judgment upon Man for his rebellion and unbridled sin. *And yet...He continued working in spite of demonic activity* (Genesis 6:3) *and the evil imaginations of Man's heart* (Genesis 6:6-7). *And, yet...Noah found grace in the eyes of the Lord* (Genesis 6:8)!

Indeed, despite Man's fallen state and God's required judgment, Scripture teaches that our God remains reluctant in His judgment.

- ☐ **God is reluctant to send Man hardships!** *For the Lord will not cast off forever: But though He cause grief, yet will He have compassion according to the multitude of His mercies. For He doth not afflict willingly nor grieve the children of men* (Lamentations 3:31-33). Because of the Fall, disease and death will come as consequences of sin. And yet, God does not delight in allowing them to impact His children.

- ☐ **God is reluctant to send Man to Hell!** *The Lord is not slack concerning His promise, as some men count slackness; but is longsuffering to us-ward, not willing that any should perish, but that all should come to repentance* (2 Peter 3:9). Because of Man's rejection of God's offer of salvation, a second death will come upon those who refuse to repent. And yet, God does not delight in allowing the lost to seal their eternal destiny!

In the life and preaching of the minister, we should be reminded of God's ministry of patience with us and with our congregation. With this in mind, we should then preach boldly with conviction, and yet, with compassion! May our preaching reflect this Reluctant God!

> *Now the God of patience and consolation grant you to be likeminded one toward another according to Christ Jesus.*
> *– Romans 15:5*

Principles and Perils of an Anointed Ministry

Unlike Moses, who put a veil over his face so that the children of Israel could not look steadily at the end of what was passing away. — 2 Corinthians 3:13 (NKJV)

Anointed preaching distinguishes New Testament preaching from all other forms of communication! Paul stated in 1 Thessalonians 1:5: *For our gospel came not unto you in word only, but also in power, and in the Holy Ghost, and in much assurance; as ye know what manner of men we were among you for your sake.* Further, in 1 Corinthians 2:4, Paul stated: *And my speech and my preaching was not with enticing words of man's wisdom, but in demonstration of the Spirit and of power.* Paul's description of Moses in 2 Corinthians 3 reveals both principles and perils of an anointed ministry. Each principle of an anointed ministry is alternated by a peril of an anointed ministry.

The Bible mentions three types of ministries: **assumed** ministries (such as Korah in Numbers 16), **appointed** ministries (such as those mentioned in Hosea 8:4), and **anointed** ministries (such as that of Moses in Exodus 34:29-35). God's purposes are best accomplished through anointed ministries! Reading from Isaiah 61:1, Jesus said, *The Spirit of the Lord is upon Me, because He hath anointed Me to preach the gospel.* Jesus embraced the principle of anointed preaching!

However, it is important to note that as the pastor ministers, there is a diminishing of that spiritual power that comes from anointing. **The Principle of Diminishing our Power through Service** is dramatically pictured as God's glory reflected in Moses' face began to diminish after his encounter on Mount Sinai when he received the Ten Commandments. This principle can also be observed in Moses at Rephidim (Exodus 17:10-12), in Jesus as He discerned that virtue had gone out of Him when He was touched by the woman with the issue of blood (Luke 8:41-48), in Elijah following his contest with false prophets on Mount Carmel (1 Kings 18-19), and in Jonah following the Ninevah revival (Jonah 4:1-11).

Preaching takes it's toll upon a person. Research has determined that a thirty-minute preaching of the gospel is estimated to equal 8 hours of hard physical labor or 12 hours of work as an executive. The strain impacts the physical, the mental, the emotional, and the spiritual being of man. When that spiritual power is diminished, the minister is at his most vulnerable point for secret, besetting, or even scandalous sins!

Evan Roberts was mightily used in the 1904 Welsh Revival, but his health took a serious crash that lasted for more than 45 years. Frequently, doctors examined him but offered no counsel. When asked by a visiting preacher if Roberts thought that anyone would rise up to lead another such revival, Roberts responded, "Who would be willing to make the sacrifice?"

The Holy Spirit's control in the preacher's life is indispensable because the anointing of the Spirit allows the listeners to hear two voices – the voice of the speaker and the voice of the Spirit! Omitting this anointing makes the message merely another oratory. With a confidence that comes from the Holy Spirit's anointing, the preacher can be assured that God will speak to the listeners. However, if the preacher is not prepared to acknowledge the principle of diminishing power through service, he becomes vulnerable to his flesh, the world, and even the devil. We must strive to maintain physical, mental, and emotional health in order to finish our ministry well.

Reminder: Our spiritual intake must always be greater than the spiritual outflow!

> *Cast me not away from thy presence; and take not thy Holy Spirit from me.* – Psalms 51:11

The alternate peril to **The Principle of Diminishing Our Power through Service** is **The Peril of Accomplishing Our Ministry without Anointing**. Paul described Moses' fleshly response to his power being diminished through his service. He did not want the people to see that diminishing, so he tried to cover it up with a veil. Rather than seeking a fresh anointing by being in the presence of God, Moses tried to continue by relying on the past! Attempting to accomplish ministry without the Spirit's anointing always leads to spiritual catastrophe in both the life of the preacher and the life of his congregation.

We live in a day in the life of the Church during which there are multiple veils a preacher can employ to cover the diminishing power brought about through his service. Extravagant programs, brag-worthy numbers, flashy personalities, and even crafty stories in place of Word-centered sermons will all produce temporal, fleshly results – but at great cost to eternal, spiritual fruit! Eternal, spiritual fruit can only come through a fresh anointing of the Holy Spirit. Sermon preparation can never substitute for servant preparation!

The tendency among ministers who have lost the anointing is to continue to serve as usual. Revivalist Leonard Ravenhill said that the worst thing his eyes had ever seen on earth was not the pagan-practicing aborigines in New Guinea, nor the destitute drug addict in the New York City alleyways; rather the worst thing his eyes had ever seen was a man of God who once had the anointing of the Holy Spirit, but had lost it and continued to serve without it!

Those who have been the most successful know what it means to attempt to serve without their discipline and diligence of daily withdrawals. Famed preacher, W.E. Sangster wrote, "Give up work if need be. Your influence finally is dependent upon your first-hand knowledge of the unseen world."

Even our Lord Jesus guarded Himself from the peril of accomplishing His ministry without the Spirit's fresh anointing. Luke 5:16 describes His discipline with these words: *And He withdrew himself into the wilderness, and prayed.* In the Greek, the words appear in the plural – many withdrawals, many wildernesses, and many prayers. Jesus' schedule gave way to His prayer life with the dividends of anointed preaching.

The well-known pianist Arthur Rubinstein confessed, "If I miss my piano practice one day, I know it; if I miss my practice two days, my friends know it; and if I miss my practice three days the whole world knows it!" Pastor, your congregation knows when you have missed the Holy Spirit's fresh anointing that comes from your consistent quiet time of Bible study and prayer. They know the difference between a sermon preached in the flesh and a message preached with the anointing of God's Spirit. Will you devalue all of your veils and guard yourself against the peril of accomplishing your ministry without that anointing?

Be challenged by Romans 15:18: *For I will not dare to speak of any of those things which Christ hath not wrought by me, to make the Gentiles obedient, by word and deed.*

Not only does Paul's reference to Moses in 2 Corinthians 2:13 reveal **The Principle of Diminishing Our Power**

Through Service, but it also reveals **The Principle of Replenishing Our Power Through Prayer**.

When Moses detected his power diminishing following his encounter with God on Mount Sinai, he eventually retreated to the Tent of Meeting to be replenished. The text of Exodus 33:9-11 is worth our investigation: *And it came to pass, as Moses entered into the Tabernacle, the cloudy pillar descended, and stood at the door of the Tabernacle, and the LORD talked with Moses. And all the people saw the cloudy pillar stand at the tabernacle door: and all the people rose up and worshipped, every man in his tent door. And the LORD spake unto Moses face to face, as a man speaketh unto his friend. And he turned again into the camp: but his servant Joshua, the son of Nun, a young man, departed not out of the Tabernacle.*

Eventually, Moses realized that the veil in which he hid himself was no substitute for hiding himself in the presence of the Lord.

As best as I can determine, Jesus sought at least 15 retreats or withdrawals in the book of Mark alone. Although He was unable fully to get away from the crowds over 50 percent of the time, He was persistent in pursuing a retreat! He knew He had to have time alone in prayer to be refreshed!

In Isaiah 50:4, the Prophet Isaiah prophesied that the Messiah would depend upon frequent replenishing: *The Lord GOD hath given Me the tongue of the learned, that I should know how to speak a word in season to him that is weary: He wakeneth morning by morning, He wakeneth Mine ear to hear as the learned.*

Isaiah was prophesying that Jesus would be as one who is learned – another word for discipled. Jesus was indeed discipled at the feet of His Father during those early morning times of prayer!

Pastor, do you find yourself meeting at the feet of the Father morning by morning to have Him awaken your ear to be discipled personally by Him? How else do you expect Him to give you the tongue of the learned that you can speak a word to those to whom you minister? He will be faithful to give you the word that is needed to minister in the specific season of your listeners' lives. Be challenged by 2 Timothy 4:2: *Preach the word; be instant in season, out of season!*

King David knew the value of being replenished by a fresh anointing. Although he had experienced the personal anointing by Samuel, the private anointing by the Elders of Judah, and the public anointing by the Elders of Israel, David yearned for a fresh anointing as expressed in Psalm 92:10: *But my horn shalt Thou exalt like the horn of an unicorn: I shall be anointed with fresh oil.* David knew that his leadership was dependent upon a fresh anointing that came through prayer!

It is recorded that Evan Roberts of the 1904 Welsh Revival came to a particular congregation. The church building was crowded with many of those attending who had been waiting for Roberts' arrival for as much as four hours! He made his way to the front row, where one seat remained for him. There he knelt and prayed for an additional three hours! Then he arose and preached a ten-minute message, and revival came upon the congregation! I often wonder if we are willing to spend three hours in prayer for every ten minutes of preaching! Also, I wonder if the lack of such commitment to prayer is the reason people are not crowding into our churches hours ahead of time to hear us preach!

Be challenged by Mark 1:35: *And in the morning, rising up a great while before day, He went out, and departed into a solitary place, and there prayed.*

Among the specific principles and perils that govern Spirit-anointed ministry, perhaps the most subtle and Satanic driven peril is **The Peril of Embellishing Our Ministry Without Reality**! When the power that comes from prayer becomes blocked by prayerlessness, the preacher falls prey to enticing substitutes that may produce false success, but will eventually result in spiritual death.

Following Moses' encounter with God on top of Mount Sinai, he experienced such a noticeable impact that he descended the mount wearing a veil over his face to cover the glory of the Lord! Over time that anointing impact diminished. Perhaps embarrassed by such a loss, Moses continued to wear the mask-like veil so that the people of Israel would not notice that the glory of the Lord had departed him! Moses sought to cover up his loss of spiritual power by wearing a mask! All along, perhaps he hoped that no one would notice!

Samson experienced a similar fate after he had succumbed to violating his Nazarite vow of not cutting his hair. Judges 16:20 states that Samson *awoke out of his sleep, and said, I will go out as at other times before, and shake myself. And he wist not that the LORD was departed from him.* Flexing his muscles, Samson did not expect anyone to notice the loss of spiritual power!

We tend to gauge spirituality based on external performance or organizational loyalty instead of internal intimacy with God! In Ezekiel 44:11 and 15 God challenged Ezekiel to observe the Temple service and note the two types of ministries: the Man-centered ministry of the majority of priests and the God-centered ministry of the High Priest Zadok! Yet, the majority of the people would never have noticed the difference!

Even in Jeremiah's day, the people of God had a difficult time distinguishing between the ministries of the true prophets and those of the false prophets. (See Jeremiah 25.) God said the difference was that His prophets rose early in the morning to meet with Him to get their message for the people of God! Earlier, the Prophet Jeremiah spoke about the false prophets who were giving out second-hand sermons, oratories, exaggerations, levities, dreams, etc., to conceal the fact that they had not risen early to meet with the Lord. (See Jeremiah 23.)

In my earlier days of ministry, I worked part-time at the Baptist Book Store on Saturdays and observed many pastors hurriedly looking for a sermon outline book to prepare for the next day's ministry. Oh, how that would break my heart, for I knew that their congregations would not be receiving a sermon prepared in the heart of the pastor as he spent time on his knees before the Lord! On Sunday, these pastors would stand in the pulpit and preach a second-hand sermon hoping that people would not notice that they had not experienced time alone with the Lord praying over the text! Pastor, there is great danger in embellishing our ministry without reality!

Be challenged by Ezekiel 44:23: *And they shall teach my people the difference between the holy and profane, and cause them to discern between the unclean and the clean.*

So far in the life of Moses, we have discovered the following principles and perils of a ministry anointed by the Holy Spirit:

- ☐ The Principle of Diminishing Our Power Through Service
- ☐ The Peril of Accomplishing Our Ministry Without Anointing

- ☐ The Principle of Replenishing Our Power Through Prayer
- ☐ The Peril of Embellishing Our Ministry Without Reality.

The epitaph ascribed to Moses in Deuteronomy 34:10 reveals a life lived in unequaled devotion: *And there arose not a prophet since in Israel like unto Moses, whom the Lord knew face to face.* Yes, Moses knew failure, but this summary of his life reveals to us **The Principle of Nourishing Our Lives Through Devotion.** Moses lived with such endurance of intimacy with the Lord that the Lord knew him face to face!

Intimacy with the Lord through prayer must become a lifestyle for the minister of God! Years from now, when you look back upon your ministry and consider a do-over, you most likely will want to change the amount of time you have spent in prayer! The noted conference speaker and author, Samuel Chadwick, wrote, "Brethren, in my ministry, I have given two-thirds of my time to Bible study and only one-third to prayer. But if I had my life to live over again, I would give two-thirds of my time to prayer and only one-third to Bible study."

When I received my doctorate, our graduation guest speaker was Herbert Lockyear, the author of over 50 books, including the wonderful *All...* series. My ministry was challenged when this 93-year-old godly man whose face radiated the Lord he served was asked what he would do differently in his ministry, knowing what he knows now. Without hesitation, Herbert Lockyear stated that he would pray more!

The Methodist Francis Asbury used to admonish his circuit riders, "When you go into the pulpit, go from your closets!" In Matthew 10:27, Jesus was quite clear about the proper source of our sermons when He said: *What I tell you in darkness, that speak ye in light: and what ye hear in the ear, that preach ye upon the housetops.* Jesus also made it clear that fruitful preaching rewarded by the Lord has its source in the prayer closet. (See Matthew 6:6.)

The revivalist Humphry Jones used to say that he would go to his prayer closet and pray. Having gotten a word from God, he would then rush to the pulpit and preach. Afterward, he would picture himself before the Judgment Seat of God to give an answer for what he had just preached!

In Jude 1:14, the Bible records that Enoch prophesied of the coming of the Lord. Hence, it is appropriate to label Enoch as the first preacher. Significantly, the Old Testament gives testimony that he walked closely with God! (See Genesis 5:22-24.)

Preaching from a prayer closet is not just a quick method for sermon preparation. It is the method for servant preparation. It is living a life nourished through the day to day devotion of intimacy with the Lord. When God calls a man to the ministry, He gives him a life-message and a life-ministry! If we deepen the life-message, God will broaden the life-ministry! Our ministry can never go beyond the measure of what has been wrought in the secret places with God on a day to day basis! Plainly stated, we will never go any further in our ministries than our devotional lives will take us!

A survey among seminary students revealed that 93 percent of those studying for the ministry did not have a consistent devotional life! Habits built in the seminary carry over into the ministry! The latest survey that I have seen reveals that the average minister spends only 7 minutes a day in prayer. May I ask, are you nourished through your enduring devotional life? Does God know you face to face?

Be challenged by 2 Corinthians 4:1: *Therefore, seeing we have this ministry, as we have received mercy, we faint not.*

Deuteronomy 34:4 brings us to the close of Moses' life: *And the Lord said unto Moses, This is the land which I share unto Abraham, unto Isaac, and unto Jacob, saying, I will give it unto thy seed: I have caused thee to see it with thine eyes, but thou shalt not go over thither.* The death of Moses reveals that he ended his life bearing the consequences of falling prey to our last peril of an anointed ministry: **The Peril of Finishing Our Ministry Without Purity.** After so many faithful years of service through nourishing his life in devotion to the Lord, it is sad to read the end of Moses' life! We do not know the length of time that Moses failed to nourish himself in the presence of the Lord before he became controlled by his anger and struck the rock at Maribah recorded in Numbers 20:9-13, but we do know that he failed to replenish that spiritual power and ended up without purity due to a prideful moment in his life. Moses ended without purity and outside the Promise Land!

Moses' failure can become our epitaph as well – unless the secret of our spiritual intimacy is maintained in full strength! One of the perils of an anointed ministry is that we can get so busy that we neglect the secret history of personally walking with God! We may end up as pure professionals! It is significant to note that just before falling into the trap of his pride, Moses sought guidance from the Lord for meeting the people's needs. (See Numbers 20:6-9.) He was faithful in his leadership role, but he failed in having that necessary role of personal intimacy with the Lord. Such a simple one-time failure, yet it kept Moses from finishing his ministry well by achieving his life goal. We must refuse any measure of activity that prevents us from our intimacy with God!

In Acts 6:4, Peter established that prayer, not preaching, is the first priority of the ministry. Building that secret intimacy with God in prayer is our foremost responsibility. What we say should never exceed what we are! Remember, we are just as commissioned to pray as we are to preach! We should be like the priests in Exodus 30, who were given the task of maintaining the fire on the altar – every morning and evening. According to Leviticus 6:13, the fire was never to go out! Ben Franklin confessed that he used to go to hear George Whitfield preach "just to watch him burn!"

We stand warned by the Israel Tribes of Reuben, Gad, and the half-tribe of Manasseh who desired their inheritance without going over the Jordan River! They wanted to be a part of the blessings of Israel, but they refused to pay the cost to be near the Tabernacle. Like many today in the ministry, they wanted the benefits of a dynamic ministry without paying the cost of maintaining a secret history with God. By remaining on the wrong side of the Jordan River, they were the first to be attacked by opposing enemies!

Oh, to God that you would embrace the principles and eliminate the perils of a ministry anointed by the Holy Spirit! In 1978, God saved my ministry from self-destructing when I made four commitments, the same four commitments that I challenge you to embrace today:

- ☐ Preach out of the prayer closet (Matthew 10:27)
- ☐ Preach from the anointing of God (Luke 4:18)
- ☐ Preach through the Word of God (2 Timothy 4:2; John 7:18)
- ☐ Preach from a life-message (Romans 15:18)

The results of these four commitments created a virtual spiritual greenhouse effect in our church!

> *I have fought a good fight, I have finished my course, I have kept the faith.* — 2 Timothy 4:7

Suffering

embracing patience that yields godliness

And to temperance, patience and to patience godliness
– 2 Peter 1:6b

CHAPTER 6

A Life-Message Illuminated by Suffering

Take, my brethren, the prophets, who have spoken in the name of the Lord, for an example of suffering affliction, and of patience. — James 5:10

In our ongoing discovery of how to apply the Biblical steps of discipleship to our lives and our preaching, we have now examined the following four steps:
- ☐ A Life-Message Initiated by Salvation
- ☐ A Life-Message Interpreted by Separation
- ☐ A Life-Message Integrated through Surrender
- ☐ A Life-Message Inspired by the Spirit.

The fifth step flows naturally out of a Spirit-anointed ministry; for Satan and the world are driven to oppose and oppress a godly ministry that is empowered by the Spirit's anointing. The Apostle Paul in 2 Timothy 3:12 stated: *Yea, and all that will live godly in Christ Jesus shall suffer persecution.* Yet the Lord does not waste the evil opposition. He uses it to bring spiritual growth and enlightenment. Through the suffering, He is more powerfully able to shine forth the message. So we now focus on **A Life-Message Illuminated by Suffering.**

Christianity takes a unique perspective that suffering is woven into the warp-and-woof of life. Preaching is not merely working up a message but is more working out the message that the preacher may be a pattern for others. In

Titus 2:7-8 Paul wrote: *In all things shewing thyself a pattern of good works: in doctrine shewing uncorruptness, gravity, sincerity, sound speech, that cannot be condemned; that he that is of the contrary part may be ashamed, having no evil thing to say of you.*

Through the pain, the hurts, and the sufferings in the ministry, the preacher develops a unique life-message. Each of the four Gospels bears the personalized mark of the individual writer. Their very life was woven into the unique fabric of the Gospel they wrote! Paul reminded us in Philippians 2:12 that we are to work out our salvation. Only what has been worked in can be worked out!

In Luke 9, Jesus instructed His disciples concerning the three tests that they would face in their ministry. Every preacher will face these tests at one time or another in his own ministry.

The Test of Ministry Hardships: *And it came to pass, that, as they went in the way, a certain man said unto Him, Lord, I will follow thee whithersoever thou goest. And Jesus said unto him, Foxes have holes, and birds of the air have nests; but the Son of man hath not where to lay His head.* (Luke 9:57-58) Jesus knew the physical exhaustion of having no place to call home to recuperate from His demanding ministry. He wanted those who followed Him to recognize the physical suffering their laboring would require. The physical and volitional drain of day by day ministering eventually takes its toll upon the preacher. Plainly stated, the ministry is filled with pressures and hardships! My first senior staff pastor, Dr. Bill Bennett, would admonish his staff, "God never calls a lazy man into the ministry!" The preacher must be prepared for exhaustion in his personal and ministerial life. But he must also have a disciplined focus to embrace the exhaustion as part of the Lord's refining him through suffering!

Be challenged by 2 Peter 3:14: *Wherefore, beloved, seeing that ye look for such things, be diligent that ye may be found of Him in peace, without spot, and blameless.*

The Test of Family Relationship: *And He said unto another, Follow Me. But he said, Lord, suffer me first to go and bury my father. Jesus said unto him, Let the dead bury their dead: but go thou and preach the kingdom of God.* (Luke 9:59-60) Jesus knew the call to the ministry significantly involves one's family. Indeed, 70 percent of the qualifications for the ministry listed in Scripture centers around the minister being a good husband and father. (See 1 Timothy 3:1-7.) God wants the preacher to model the message before his congregation by living it out among his family. This domestic focus will force the minister to make priority choices socially and spiritually. Pastor, do you place a high priority on discipling and leading your family by enlisting their participation in God's work? When they have embraced the concept that they are an indispensable element in the Lord's work by serving with you, you, as a family, can be faithful to proper priorities without offense.

Be challenged by Ephesians 6:4: *And ye fathers, provoke not your children to wrath, but bring them up in the nurture and admonition of the Lord.*

The Test of Submissive Stewardship: *And another also said, Lord, I will follow thee; but let me first go bid them farewell, which are at home at my house. And Jesus said unto him, No man, having put his hand to the plough, and looking back, is fit for the kingdom of God.* (Luke 9:61-62) Jesus realized the mental, emotional, and financial drain that the call to the ministry requires. This call means being faithful in the furrows and remaining optimistic even when there is a lack of financial resources. This determined focus may make or break the minister. Pastor, do you stay faithful to your calling when all looks bleak? Will you learn to trust the Lord for the necessary financial means to conduct your ministry?

Be challenged by Philippians 4:19: *But my God shall supply all your needs according to His riches in glory by Christ Jesus.*

Each of these three areas of testing in the ministry (ministry hardship, family relationship, and submissive stewardship) is a window of opportunity to renew one's commitment and calling to the Lord's service! Unless the preacher is faithful in utilizing each of these three areas of suffering to enhance his life-message, he will not be successful in his calling!

Jesus faced all three of these tests Himself and left us an example to follow! In 1 Peter 2:21, Peter declares, *For even hereunto were ye called: because Christ also suffered for us, leaving us an example, that ye should follow His steps.* He, too, faced the test of ministry hardship through an exhausting schedule with nowhere to lay His head! He, too, faced the test of family relationship when His family questioned even His sanity and His calling! He, too, faced the test of submissive stewardship when He even lacked the money to pay His taxes! Jesus built a life-message illuminated by suffering (see Isaiah 53), and He bids each of us to follow His example!

> *That I may know Him, and the power of His resurrection, and the fellowship of His sufferings, being made conformable unto His death.* – Philippians 3:10

Suffering Through Opposition

> *Then assembled together the chief priests, and the scribes, and the elders of the people, unto the palace of the high priest, who was called Caiaphas, And consulted that they might take Jesus by subtilty, and kill Him.* — Matthew 26:3-4

Many pastors fail to recognize that they are pastoring several groups of people and not just one congregation! The Apostle Paul wrote in 1 Corinthians 12:14, 18: *For the body is not one member, but many. But now hath God set the members every one of them in the body, as it hath pleased Him.* Failure to recognize this understanding of variety within the body of Christ will lead to conflicts with the pastor's leadership and confusion concerning the focus of the pastor's messages.

During the time of Jesus, there existed at least six groups within Judaism who held differing perspectives of God's Word:

- **Herodians** – Liberal Activists who embraced an Hellenistic, evolutionary worldview
- **Sadducees** – A Control Group of wealthy people from prominent, priestly families
- **Scribes** – Experts on the Law, both as transcribers and interpreters
- **Pharisees** – Law Legalists who sought to live by rules while split over well-noted teachers
- **Zealots** – A Rebellious Group who were more interested in tradition than God's truth
- **Essenes** – An Isolationist Group whose end-time view made social and moral culture distasteful.

When Jesus called the Twelve Disciples, He chose a diverse lot! It appears that Jesus selected a disciple or two from each of the above groups within Judaism. Matthew was from a Levite family but worked for the Herodians.

Nathaniel and Philip were Scribes. Simon and Judas were Zealots. Andrew, John, and James, all followers of John the Baptist, were influenced by the Essenes. Thomas was likely a Sadducee. And James the Less, Peter, and Thaddeus may have been Pharisees. We cannot strongly affirm that they belonged to these particular groups, but their various connections seem to indicate that Jesus was purposely selecting them as representatives.

It is important to note that Jesus Himself did not fit with any of the Jewish systems of interpreting Scripture! He came to fulfill the Law, not lend his Name to any particular group. Matthew 22 reveals that each of these groups united in their opposition to Jesus at the end of Jesus' ministry! They all joined to have Jesus executed. Luke 6:11 seems to imply that there was a Satanic unification to oppose Jesus: *And they were filled with madness; and communed one with another what they might do to Jesus.*

Pastor, if you have opposition within your church, you are not alone! Jesus, the Apostles, and church leaders throughout history have all had opposition. God, however, wants you to minister to the diversity within the Body of Christ. In doing so, your messages must become varied! They should not reflect a bias against any particular group. When one group opposes your ministry, you must not turn your supporters against your opposers. Guard against being a people-pleaser and taking sides in response to opposition toward you! Train yourself to recognize opposition as an opportunity to suffer for your refining!

(For further insights, please see the following Scriptures: Mark 8:15; Matthew 16:6, 11; Mark 12:38; Luke 12:1; Matthew 26:52; John 17:15.)

> *And these things, brethren, I have in a figure transferred to myself and to Apollos for your sakes; that ye might learn in us*

not to think of men above that which is written, that no one of you be puffed up for one against another. – 1 Corinthians 4:6

Suffering Through Rising Opposition

They shall put you out of the synagogues: yea, the time cometh, that whosoever killeth you will think that he doeth God service.   — John 16:2

Jesus lamented in Matthew 23:37: *O Jerusalem, Jerusalem, thou that killest the prophets, and stonest them which are sent unto thee, how often would I have gathered thy children together, even as a hen gathereth her chickens under her wings, and ye would not!* His lament acknowledges that opposition to God's righteous preacher is not new. Such opposition or persecution has been happening from the beginning, even with Cain and Abel! (See Matthew 23:35 and Luke 11:51.) Generations of covenant brothers have become church brothers, but not much has changed. There are still those within the congregation who subtly or openly oppose God's man!

Paul and Robert Schenick, in their book, *The Extermination of Christianity – a Tyranny of Consensus*, have identified a familiar five-step process of opposition. It is a process that is noticeable throughout history and is clearly seen in the book of Daniel:

1. **Identify and stereotype the target person or group** (Daniel 1:3,4) The captured Israelites were identified as gifted above all others in appearance, leadership skills, wisdom, knowledge, and understanding. *Lesson*: The opposition will first identify the righteous who do not fit into their control group. They will be uncomfortable with the challenge their righteousness brings. Then

they will, in turn, stereotype the righteous who do not conform to their ways.
2. **Marginalize the target person or group from the mainstream** (Daniel 1:5-7) The captured Israelites were separated for three years with controlled diets and attempts to change their language and identity by changing their names from Hebrew to Chaldean. *Lesson*: The opposition will then seek to limit the influence and impact of the righteous who do not assimilate or conform to their group by exaggerating their uniqueness.
3. **Vilify the target person or group as a threat** (Daniel 1:20-2:49) The captured Israelites were ten times more skilled than the other choice influencers of the king and yet they were accused of lying and corruption. *Lesson*: Ridiculing and belittling the righteous through false accusations creates a climate of distrust and a justification for abuse.
4. **Criminalize the target person or group by discriminatory restrictions** (Daniel 3:1-12) The captured Israelites were entrapped by the decree that all who did not bow down to the king's idol would be thrown into a fiery furnace. Note the punishment came from the threatened herald, not from the king's direction. However, when the king was disobeyed, his fury dictated his enforcement. *Lesson*: Placing compromising requirements or demands upon the righteous will place them under a false standard that will be impossible to maintain. Thus, the righteous will eventually cross a line, which justifies a response by the opposition.
5. **Exterminate or eliminate the target person or group** (Daniel 3:19-22) The captured Israelites were bound and put in the fiery furnace that was made seven

times hotter. ***Lesson***: Finally, the righteous must be removed by force from the midst of the opposition.

This destructive pattern of persecution can be seen today in many congregations as well as in cultural clashes. It is heart-rending to observe a pastor treated this way by a congregation, but it does happen. Pastor, you must recognize the dynamics of the growing opposition. There are few surprises here! Satan is not creative. He continues to use a pattern that has been most effective throughout history.

Be encouraged by the patriarch Joseph's assurance stated in Genesis 50:20: *But as for you, ye thought evil against me; but God meant it unto good, to bring to pass, as it is this day, to save much people alive.* Being opposed does not reflect weakness or unfaithfulness on the part of the righteous preacher! But God does desire that such suffering builds character and, then, in turn, a message!

> *Therefore I endure all things for the elect's sakes, that they may also obtain the salvation which is in Christ Jesus with eternal glory.* — 2 Timothy 2:10

Seasons of Suffering

> *Preach the Word; be instant in season, out of season; reprove, rebuke, exhort with all longsuffering and doctrine.*
> — 2 Timothy 4:2

While personal suffering is the Holy Spirit's method of working the message into the preacher's life, the suffering of the congregation should also have a significant impact upon the preacher's sermons. Paul challenged Timothy to preach the Word in season and out of season by exhorting in all long-suffering.

King Solomon began Ecclesiastes chapter three with the statement: *To every thing there is a season, and a time to every purpose under the heaven.* He then proceeded to list 14 seasons of human life with their raw emotional terminus points of beginnings and endings. At times he moved through these from delightful moments to disquieting moments, but then at other times, he reversed and moved from disquieting moments to delightful moments. Most of life is lived in between these 14 seasons of beginnings and endings. Yet we all experience the emotional moments of the beginnings and endings!

Pastor, you and I have been called to minister to people both "in between" and "during" these emotional events of their lives. We are called to bring a message of hope, love, and forgiveness to those who are suffering. We are to bring the Immanuel (*God with us*) into their moments of joy and fulfillment. Life "under the sun" lived on this side of the Curse of Eden guarantees the knowledge of the joys of *good* and the pain of *evil*. We are to help people understand and discern the difference between good and evil, holy and profane, clean and unclean. (See Ezekiel 44:23.)

Our task in preaching is to motivate people to move from the *Curse of the Fall* to the *Covenant of Faith* and from life *under the sun* to life *under heaven*. (See Ecclesiastes 1:3 and 1:13.)

As those who are called to preach God's Word, we must make ourselves familiar with these events and train ourselves to be sensitive to the specific needs during them. May we help people to work out their faith with doctrinal clarity in each of the 14 seasons of human life.

A time to be born, and a time to die;   – Ecclesiastes 3:2

As pastors, we must be ready to celebrate the birth of a new life! This is a high point in the life of a husband and wife and of a family unit. But birth has its stressful times as each birth reminds us of our own fragile existence and the death of loved ones who are no longer with us to experience such joy. Birth represents a new beginning, and it is no wonder Jesus used the topic of birth to teach us about the new birth. We must understand creation and birth if we are to understand the new creation and the new birth.

Pastors must be ready to minister to those at the other end of life — the time to die! We should never look into a casket or a grave without allowing it to change us! It is so sad that today's secular influence has impacted Christian funerals so that we have turned the occasion into a time of joyful reminiscence instead of a time of serious reconsiderations. Eternity is on the other side of death, and pastors need to utilize the occasion to call people to examine their state. For those who remain behind, death is often filled with pain, grief, guilt, regrets, and loss.

A time to plant, and a time to pluck up that which is planted;
– Ecclesiastes 3:2

Planting in an agricultural environment is often the same as searching for a job in an urban environment. Both are stressful, arduous times. Questions of timing, of watering, of resume preparations, and of job interviews are indeed stressful moments that turn into weeks or months of uncertainty. Those who go through these testing times need to know how to find God's will and purpose for their lives.

Life's harvest time could mean a time of retirement, although most preachers never really retire! However, there comes a time when the discipler-pastor must step aside and allow the next generation to take over the full responsibilities of pastoring. We must learn to be gracious when that time comes. The adjustment may be difficult for many, but a wise pastor will accept this time of "finishing my course" and become more of an intercessor and encourager behind the scenes.

A time to kill, and a time to heal; — Ecclesiastes 3:3

To the farmer, there is a time to kill off livestock or to thin out the herd. There is time to bring to an end the life of the plants. Man was given the responsibility of dominion over the life of the animals. There are times when the price of the Fall means death – timely or untimely. Man oversees so much of this as it fits within God's will. There are also times that are marked by deadly catastrophes and calamities. These are difficult occasions in which to minister. The pastor must feel the hurt that is beyond his understanding. During those times when one cannot understand the hand of God, he must learn to trust His heart. Are we prepared to help those who must walk through the Valley of Death? Are we prepared to minister at death's door when a baby is miscarried, a youth dies tragically in a senseless act of foolishness, or an accident that robbed us of some of our finest heroes?

There are also times of healing. Oh, how we at times fight against healing – to take our medicine, to take our rest, to eat less, and to exercise more! Without times of healing, there is only sickness and death. There must be times of healing! From the Lord, there is the oil of healing as surely as a shepherd would anoint the head of a wounded lamb. As pastors, we must therapeutically minister to those who need healing. Do we know what to say when the tragic news comes, for example, that dreaded word, "cancer"? Are we ready to be healers?

A time to break down, and a time to build up;
– Ecclesiastes 3:3

Life also involves becoming broken. When pride takes someone too far, and one must become broken and repentant, will we be there to aid them through that crisis? When all has gone wrong, and a person finds himself "feeding the pigs" of life, will we be there to tell them how to find their way back to the Father's house?

Edification is a word not often used today, but it means to build up, to strengthen. One of the great roles of a pastor is to edify and strengthen those who have been beaten down by life! Some are at the lowest rung of the ladder when they should be at the top! Life has treated them so unfairly. Like the publican in the Temple, they can no longer look up to God! Pastors must help them through this trying time and build their confidence back up!

A time to weep, and a time to laugh;   – Ecclesiastes 3:4

Weeping is difficult for so many! To them, it is a sign of weakness, but nothing is further from the truth. Man must weep for a season! God collects our tears in a bottle. In eternity, God will reveal how each tear was preserved! He knew and understood those testing times. At times, we say to others, "get a good cry." Weeping is therapeutic. It is the body's way of detoxing harmful chemicals brought on by stressful emotions. Weeping should be shared. As pastors, do we have a shoulders on which people may weep?

Jesus loved a good laugh! His sense of humor comes through in His parables and in His illustrations of life! Laughter is also therapeutic. Proverbs teaches that laughter is good medicine (Proverbs 17:22). A good laugh brings out creativity and joy. Why is it that so many view Christianity as a "down in the mouth" type of religion? It should be just the opposite!

A time to mourn, and a time to dance;   – Ecclesiastes 3:4

The Jewish people established traditions around mourning – what to wear and for how long, whether to fast and for how long, and whether to cover their hair with ashes or not. There were mourning customs for most of our heritages, but it is seldom considered today. Mourning? Get over it! Well, that is how some people feel. How long should one mourn over the loss of a parent, or a spouse, or an offspring? Perhaps there are no set time limits, but there should be an extended time to work through that mourning period. As pastors, we must be empathetic.

Time to dance? For the conservative Baptist, this may be the greatest challenge on the list! King David danced before the Lord. Perhaps, he was not a Baptist! Seriously, David danced before the Lord because the Ark of the Covenant had arrived at the Holy Place! The Jewish People dance often and often in times of worship. For David, this was a time of celebrating and dancing. Are we prepared to "dance" with others in their times of celebration?

A time to cast away stones, and a time to gather stones together;   – Ecclesiastes 3:5

For the farmer, stones in the field at plowing time become real obstacles that must be removed. There are times in our lives when "stones," things that hinder us, must be removed. Stones are good for walls and buildings, but not for plowed fields. Too often, people in our congregations have stones that hinder their growth. As a pastor, are we prepared to help people remove those hindrances? Are we willing to be bold in our preaching to remove stumbling blocks and strongholds from people's lives?

There are also times of gathering stones for building! Do we know the building stones of discipleship? Are we prepared to walk people through these stepping stones to a victorious, mature Christian life? Are we prepared to defend the faith and put up a stone wall of defense?

A time to embrace, and a time to refrain from embracing;
– Ecclesiastes 3:5

There are times when an embrace or a touch says more than a hundred sermons! How reassuring is the embrace from a brother in Christ whom we have not seen for many years! How comforting is the hug when the weight of a crisis crushes someone. Are we as pastors so aloof and cold as to deny a needed embrace? Do we offer a cold-shoulder instead of a shoulder to lean on?

Embracing can go too far! Some don't like to be touched, and some like to be touched too much! There are boundaries that should not be crossed! Like Job's friends, there are times when we may just sit with the hurting person and not be in such a hurry to embrace or touch. True enough, Jesus often "touched" the lepers and the ill. I often wonder if that touch was in the form of an embrace.

A time to get, and a time to lose;   – Ecclesiastes 3:6

We are living in a day when many do not know how to be good losers! This is true on a grand scale from a Presidential election to a Super Bowl game. But this attitude rises from a much lower level. We want to reward those who just show up! Trophies are given to everyone! There are no losers! At least that is what many in our society think today.

However, the truth is that if we are going to be a winner, then we will also be a loser somewhere along the way. The greater the win, the greater the loss. As pastor, we must be there for those who suffer the greatest of losses in life. This may be the loss of a spouse through death or divorce, the loss of a job, the loss of one's health, the loss of a child, or the loss of one's house due to fire. These losses are devastating, and the pastor must minister to those in suffering. He must also minister to his own losses in life. Please note, a congregation is watching us to see how we handle our losses.

A time to keep, and a time to cast away; – Ecclesiastes 3:6

There are those who are hoarders of things that are not healthy, but I think Solomon has in mind the responsibility upon our shoulders to be good custodians of what has been given to us. We must be willing to do the needed maintenance of those things that the Lord has given to us! We must be responsible for the heirlooms, the inheritances, the good things of the Lord. As pastors, we should be prepared to help people to recognize their responsibilities to be good stewards of what the Lord has given.

Being a good steward also involves disposal. Without a doubt, there are "things" in our lives that we need to cast away! If you have lived in the same house for over, say, thirty years, you have accumulated a lot of stuff! Downsizing and getting rid of stuff that should have been discarded decades ago is mentally healthy. But perhaps, Solomon has something deeper in mind here. There is a time to cast aside old habits, old memories, old grudges, and old emotional hangups. Time to take these to the trash bin and throw them away! Pastors should help people find victory over those things in their lives.

A time to rend, and a time to sew;   – Ecclesiastes 3:7

At a dramatic crisis, the Jewish People would rend their clothes to show the raw emotions of the event. There will be those times of raw emotions, of rending! This tearing represents a departure from the status quo. It requires a new set of clothes. There must be a time of rending from old habits and old paths. As pastors, we must help people to see the clear choices they must make if they are to walk in newness of life!

My mother could sew – needlepoint, quilts, or darning a pair of socks – you name it! Our family continues to enjoy the fruit of her skill, even in her absence. Sewing is such a beautiful art, and it demands skillful coordination of eye and hand. The Bible speaks about not sewing a new garment together with an older one. They will eventually become separated again. As pastors, we too must be in the mending business. We must have such skill as to sew together any rift within the congregation or conflict within a family. If we just patch-up a situation, the job of mending these situations will merely rip apart again, and the next opportunity, perhaps, will be more severe than the previous one.

A time to keep silent, and a time to speak;
— Ecclesiastes 3:7

Clearly, there are times when it is prudent to keep one's mouth shut or not to speak. To speak may mean to lose one's job, or to jeopardize one's physical safety. At times, as a pastor who is commissioned to speak, remaining silent may be the wisest choice of action. Perhaps at a later time, he may be able to address a needed situation.

On the other hand, there are times when we must speak up. We must speak up, for example, for the unborn in a culture of abortion. We must speak up for the abused child or spouse. We must speak out for the widow who has been victimized by a financial scam.

A time to love, and a time to hate; — Ecclesiastes 3:8

Love is a strong, passionate word and, at the same time, a gentle and warm word. Many are those in our congregations who are love-starved! They wonder, is there anyone who cares? Does anyone listen? Is there love in the world? They may wonder if anyone can truly love without ulterior motives! Can we minister to them from the basis of Christ's love toward us?

Hate is another strong word, but one that lacks any gentility. Can there be any redemption with this word? Yes, we should hate the sins that caused Christ to die on a cross. We should hate the deplorable sins and conditions that destroy families and friendships. We should hate the sins without hating the sinner. No doubt, the pastor will be accused of being a hate-monger of some social sin as he makes a stand against the sin, but in reality, he is making a stand because he hates the sin, not the sinner! His stand is one of love!

A time of war, and a time of peace.   – Ecclesiastes 3:8

Solomon brings his list down to war and peace. Is there ever a war that is justified? Philosophers and theologians have wrestled with this concept. Here, by divine inspiration, God says that there are exceptional situations that will be resolved only through war. God commissioned His representative judges and kings to lead the Israelites into war. There are evil, demon-inspired leaders who raise armies to war against God's Son and His followers. It has always been so. In a time of judgment, there is time for war. Are we as pastors prepared to minister to the family with the death of a son or daughter or spouse soldier who has died in service of country?

Solomon began his listing of the various seasons in life with birth, and he ends with peace! We desire peace in the world, whether it is the global world or just our own little small world, we desire peace. Indeed, in a spiritual sense, we are born to be peacemakers in a world that is filled with war and divisions. As a pastor, are you prepared to be a peacemaker throughout the seasons of life amidst the conflicts within your congregation, or within your own family?

So teach us to number our days, that we may apply our hearts unto wisdom.   – Psalm 90:12

Sensitivity

embracing brotherly kindness

And to godliness, brotherly kindness – 2 Peter 1:7

CHAPTER 7

Having Compassion, Making a Difference

And Jesus, when He came out, saw much people, and was moved with compassion toward them, because they were as sheep not having a shepherd: and He began to teach them many things. — Mark 6:34

"It was the best of times, it was the worst of times, it was the age of wisdom, it was the age of foolishness, it was the epoch of belief, it was the epoch of incredulity..." These are the opening lines of Charles Dickens' famous novel about the French Revolution, *A Tale of Two Cities*. Dickens' words describe my feeling upon accepting my first post-seminary pastorate! I had just graduated with two degrees from two of the finest academic institutions in our country. Yet upon graduation, I discovered the Lord leading me to pastor one of the mission churches of First Baptist Church, Dallas, Texas. I went from my high educational setting to a congregation comprised of church members from inner-city housing projects and homesteads who averaged a sixth-grade education! The Missions Director told me that he expected me to burn out in less than a year. He said that I would learn more in six months at this church than I would in six years in a "normal" church! I lasted for three and one-half years not so much because I could teach and preach, but because I had learned to show compassion.

I think Dickens' words also describe how the disciples must have felt in Mark 6 when they saw a great crowd of people that had gathered! The disciples counseled Jesus to send the people away! They were often critical of the masses and were filled with condemnation. Jesus, however, was filled with compassion!

Concerning the man born blind, the disciples contended that sin caused his blindness. Additionally, when a tower fell, and several people were tragically killed, the disciples assumed that those who died were the worst of sinners. Jesus was continually correcting their attitude! He was moving them along from condemnation to compassion.

The disciples were like many today who say they are "prophets" and hurl condemnations because they only see people in black and white terms! No, people come in many colors and with many hurts, disappointments, and addictions. They are like an animal caught in a vicious snare – desperately crying out for help, for release. We must remember that people in our congregations, caught in Satan's trap, are crying out for help, for compassion, not condemnation.

Thus, we move our focus from suffering to lessons on sensitivity. If we are going to reach people where they are, we need to preach with compassion. Before I went to seminary, I spent two hours with Dr. R.G. Lee, former pastor of Bellevue Baptist Church in Memphis, TN. I asked him, if he were to do his ministry over again, what would he do differently. He said that he would preach more on love and less on judgment! How like Jesus was his answer!

> *Keep yourselves in the love of God, looking for the mercy of our Lord Jesus Christ unto eternal life. And of some have compassion, making a difference: And others save with fear, pulling them out of the fire; hating even the garment spotted by the flesh.*   – Jude 21-23

A Life-Message Intensified to Sensitivity

Preach the Word: be instant in season, and out of season; reprove, rebuke, exhort with all longsuffering and doctrine. But watch thou in all things, endure afflictions, do the work of an evangelist, make full proof of thy ministry.
— 2 Timothy 4:2, 5

Preaching should not be static. We must approach preaching with the expectation that it reflects our ever-maturing walk with the Lord. We have previously explored the following steps often repeated in Scripture that describe the process of developing a life-message through spiritual maturity and, in turn, discipling others:

- ☐ A Life-Message Initiated by Salvation
- ☐ A Life-Message Interpreted by Separation
- ☐ A Life-Message Integrated through Surrender
- ☐ A Life-Message Inspired by the Spirit
- ☐ A Life Message Illuminated by Suffering.

In God's design for the ministry, He allows the preacher to face suffering so that he can be a pattern for others who suffer, but also so that he can be in a position to identify with the needs of his congregation. After considering a ministry and a message flowing out of suffering, we come to the next step of Biblical discipleship: **A Life-Message Intensified to *Sensitivity*.**

In Luke, Jesus introduced His ministry to His needy listeners in the synagogue of Nazareth by reading from the Old Testament Book of Isaiah:

"The Spirit of the Lord is upon me, because He hath anointed me to preach the gospel to the poor; He hath sent me to heal the broken-hearted, to preach deliverance to the captives, and recovering of sight to the blind, to set at liberty them that are

> *bruised, To preach the acceptable year of the Lord." And He closed the book, and He gave it again to the minister, and sat down. And the eyes of all them that were in the synagogue were fastened on Him. And He began to say unto them, "This day is this Scripture fulfilled in your ears."* — Luke 4:18-21

Jesus was sensitive to the needs of those around Him. As a Man of Sorrows and acquainted with grief (see Isaiah 53:3), He felt the depression and the despair in the lives of those around Him. From this marvelous text in Luke, Jesus defined six needs within humanity that He intended to touch.

- ☐ **The Financially Bankrupt** *(to preach the gospel to the poor)* - To those who were *hopeless* and caught in the cycle of poverty, Jesus offered a *future* by what is often called redemption and lift.
- ☐ **The Emotionally Broken-hearted** *(to heal the broken-hearted)* - To those who were *heart-broken* and depressed, Jesus offered *friendship* and love.
- ☐ **The Morally Bound** *(to preach deliverance to the captives)* - To those who were *hapless* and miserable, Jesus offered *freedom* from the moral snares of the enemy.
- ☐ **The Willfully Blind** *(recovering of the sight to the blind)* - To those who were *helpless* and undiscerning, Jesus offered *foresight* by giving them a purpose for living.
- ☐ **The Socially Bruised** *(to set at liberty them that are bruised)* - To those who were *health-less* and devastated, Jesus offered *forgiveness* and healing both within and without.
- ☐ **The Spiritually Believing** *(to preach the acceptable year of the Lord)* - To those who were *hero-less* and confused, Jesus offered *faith* in a Shepherd for their daily life.

Indeed, Jesus was sensitive to the desperate needs of His listeners – even though many of them may not have been keenly aware of their actual condition. As the preacher embraces his suffering, he will develop a sensitivity and a discernment that will allow him to minister to the needs of his congregation as never before!

> *For even hereunto were ye called: because Christ also suffered for us, leaving us an example, that ye should follow His steps.* – 1 Peter 2:21

Are You Sensitive?

> *Shouldest not thou also have had compassion on thy fellow servant, even as I had pity on thee?* — Matthew 18:33

In the third chapter of Acts, as Peter and John approached the Temple, they found themselves surrounded by scores of needy people gathered along the streets. Since giving to the poor was considered a gracious act as one approached the Temple for worship, most of the crowd the apostles encountered would have been crying out for a donation. Out of the tumult, the Bible states that Peter and John fastened their eyes upon one beggar in particular. In response to his appeal for a donation, Peter said, *Silver and gold have I none; but such as I have give I thee: In the name of Jesus Christ of Nazareth rise up and walk* (Acts 3:4 and 6). While many would have tried to dodge all the clamor, what allowed the Holy Spirit to quicken Peter and John to be sensitive to the needs of this particular beggar?

Jesus had modeled a lifestyle of sensitivity before His disciples. He was sensitive to the children when the Disciples would have turned them away. He was sensitive to the woman at the well when the Disciples were offended by her presence. He was sensitive to the woman anointing His feet with oil when the host of the house was not. Jesus was sensitive to blind Bartimaeus and Zacchaeus up in a tree. He was sensitive to a woman touching the hem of His garment, to the lepers, to the blind, to the crippled, to the deaf, to the deformed, and to the hundreds of others that He healed throughout His ministry! While others would have simply ignored or pushed them aside, Jesus was keenly aware of their presence and their needs.

Not only had Peter and John observed Jesus modeling a lifestyle of sensitivity, but they had also been the recipients of His ministering sensitivity! When Peter was overwhelmed with the guilt of having denied his Friend and Savior, Jesus was sensitive to meet his need. When John had argued in competition with his brother, Jesus was sensitive to meet his need. Jesus' pity in the lives of both of these men when they were suffering equipped them to have compassion for a fellow servant!

In order to preach effectively in sensitivity to the needs of a congregation, the preacher must maintain a fresh gratitude for the Lord's sensitivity he has experienced through his salvation and daily sufferings. His preaching must reflect the heart of Jesus both to recognize the individual needs and to express compassion.

Is there someone today that God has placed in your path? Perhaps this person is bitter at life, suicidal through a deep depression, or lonely because of rejection. Will you be intensified through your own suffering to be sensitive to their need? As Saint Francis of Assisi instructed his followers, "Preach the Word. And if you have to, use words."

> *But thou, O Lord, art a God full of compassion, and gracious, longsuffering, and plenteous in mercy and truth.*
> *– Psalm 86:15*

The Role of Sensitivity in Our Epistle

> *Ye are our epistle written in our hearts, known and read of all men: Forasmuch as ye are manifestly declared to be the epistle of Christ ministered by us, written not with ink, but with the Spirit of the living God; not in tables of stone, but in fleshy tables of the heart.* — 2 Corinthians 2:2-3

In writing to the Corinthians, the Apostle Paul stated a principle that must be lived out in our lives, especially in the lives of those who preach the Word. We must become what we desire to preach! God's Word must be worked into our hearts and then worked out through our lives – and voices. As Paul put it, we become the epistle of Christ written by the Spirit of God that will, in turn, be known and read of all men! A message built in a life will impact a life.

Paul's words are ominous and challenging, but when broken down and understood by other verses of Scripture, the concept becomes clear. We must become sensitive to the needs of those with whom we minister. Please note the emphasis by the Holy Spirit as revealed by the repeated phrase, one another.

- ☐ We are to forgive one another as Christ forgives us. (Colossians 3:13)
- ☐ We are to forbear one another as Christ forbears with us. (Colossians 3:13)
- ☐ We are to honor one another as Christ honors us. (Romans 12:10)
- ☐ We are to be kind to one another as Christ is kind to us. (Romans 12:10)
- ☐ We are to comfort one another as Christ comforts us. (1 Thessalonians 4:18)
- ☐ We are to edify one another as Christ edifies us. (1 Thessalonians 5:11)

☐ We are to love one another as Christ loves us. (John 13:34)

The preacher must move from inside his study and church office out into the community and his congregation. He must become one of the "one-anothers" and exemplify the message he has preached. Indeed, it is through being with others that he learns and understands their hurts and needs. Afterward, the preacher is able to put flesh onto his message.

Jesus left us His example by incarnating His message. The Word became flesh and dwelt among us, becoming one of us. He was and is touched by our feelings, our hurts, and our struggles! Likewise, the preacher must flesh out his message until that message is not only heard but, as Paul states it, read by others.

> *For we have not an high priest which cannot be touched with the feeling of our infirmities; but was in all points tempted like as we are, yet without sin.* — Hebrews 4:15

Preparing to Speak the Oracles of God

> *But the end of all things is at hand: be ye therefore sober, and watch unto prayer. And above all things have fervent charity among yourselves: for charity shall cover the multitude of sins. Use hospitality one to another without grudging. As every man hath received the gift, even so minister the same one to another, as good stewards of the manifold grace of God. If any man speak, let him speak as the oracles of God; if any man minister, let him do it as of the ability which God giveth: that God in all things may be glorified through Jesus Christ, to whom be praise and dominion for ever and ever. Amen.*
> — 1 Peter 4:7-11

Peter wrote his first epistle to believers who were oppressed. He sought to console them and to give them hope!

Toward the end of his epistle, Peter became very practical in his counsel, as evidenced in the portion of his fourth chapter printed above. His forward-looking, wise counsel is for those of us who minister to the oppressed and suffering in these last days.

- We must maintain a life of **Vigilant Prayer**! (1 Peter 4:7) Our ministry must derive from a life of prayer to be effective. Anything less would be a ministry done in the flesh. But we must be vigilant and serious about our prayer life if we intend to be effective eternally. In these end-times, perhaps prayer will be the element that assures us of our very survival!
- We must maintain a life of **Fervent Love**! (1 Peter 4:8) Our ministry ought to flow out of love for our brothers and sisters in the Lord, as well as out of our love for our family. During stressful times, love must prevail, and we must be willing to place others first. With so much betrayal and covenant-breaking today, there is an overwhelming need to demonstrate love. Our love must not become cold!
- We must maintain a life of **Diligent Hospitality**! (1 Peter 4:9) How odd this sounds when directed to men in leadership, but we should, along with our wives, be diligent in providing hospitality to those who are less fortunate and who have perhaps suffered the loss of income during times of hardship. Peter gets very practical for many who are jobless or struggling to make ends meet.
- We must maintain a life of **Obedient Stewardship**! (1 Peter 4:10) Our ministry may not rise to the level that we think it ought to achieve, but one thing that we can be is obedient stewards to discharge our responsibilities where and when the Lord places us

in His providentially-chosen opportunities. God has blessed us with such wealth that billions throughout the world do not enjoy. He expects us to use His blessings to sustain and bless others.

☐ We must maintain a life of **Consistent Speaking**! (1 Peter 4:11) With the first four considerations in place, Peter now addressed the speaking or preaching of God's called servant. It should be out of a message built in a life that we have a life message to deliver to others. God does not call the qualified, but, instead, He qualifies the called with His anointing so that He may be eternally glorified in all things!

The preacher who wants to disciple must focus upon being sensitive to the suffering of others. Don't waste *your* suffering! Employ your suffering as a tool to develop sensitivity! Allow your suffering to shape your ministry and give you opportunities to serve and speak with sensitivity to those who are hurting!

> *Now we exhort you, brethren, warn them that are unruly, comfort the feebleminded, support the weak, be patient toward all men.* – 1 Thessalonians 5:14

Spirituality

embracing love

And to brotherly kindness, charity
– 2 Peter 1:7

CHAPTER 8

Life-Message Incarnated by Spirituality

And now abideth faith, hope, charity, these three; but the greatest of these is charity.   — 1 Corinthians 13:13

The ultimate goal of discipleship is true **spirituality** that is governed by love! God begins with our **salvation** through which He calls us to **separation**. Then He brings us to **surrender** to His Word in all our commitments and decisions. As we surrender, we discover our utter dependence upon **Spirit-control** to be successful. God then allows **suffering** through the opposition of the enemy to shape us, graced with increased **sensitivity** to the needs of others. As that sensitivity becomes a way of life, we begin to reflect the very nature of God Who is love! God Himself is incarnated into our very being. By God's grace, we have a **Life-Message Incarnated into Spirituality**!

As previously mentioned, before going to seminary, my life was impacted by the wonderful occasion of spending a couple of hours with Dr. R.G. Lee, pastor of Bellevue Baptist Church in Memphis, Tennessee, for 33 years and three-term president of the Southern Baptist Convention. As my time was drawing to the end, I asked Dr. Lee, "If you were to do your ministry over again, knowing what you know now, what would you differently?" He responded, "I would preach less on judgment and more on love." The goal of the preacher's life is not a higher position in the church nor a collection of certificates of achievement and accolades. The goal is love, plain and simple!

From a Biblical perspective and with New Testament discernment, this love is unique to Christianity. This agapé-type of love is selfless and God-centered! This love is totally different from the loves that the world and its religions have to offer! Oh, how this love is missing from our pulpits!

In reality, the Greeks emphasized various kinds of love, each of which centered around a different Greek word. These various shades of love should be in the life of the preacher, the focus of his counseling, and the passion of his preaching:

Storgé (στοργή) describes family love. This word is used to describe the stable love that should exist within the family structure. It pictures the beautiful love between a husband and wife, between parent and child, and between siblings. It provides security and confidence. This love is so needed in our families today!

Phileó (φιλέω) describes friendship love. This love describes the wonderful friendship between two individuals. It involves commitment and fellowship. Plato spoke of it as being respectful and admirable.

Epithumia (ἐπιθυμία) describes emotional love. The word is used to express strong cravings and motivation to achieve. This word is not used in the Bible. Selfish drives govern mere emotional love. The term can be misused and have the connotations of coveting or lusting after something.

Eros (ἔρως) describes romantic love. More than the other words for love, this word carries with it the strong, passionate love. True romance today has unfortunately soured and has diminished in connotation to that of sexual love.

Agapé (ἀγάπη) describes Christ-like love. The Greek word was radically changed by the New Testament writers and was used to describe divine or totally unselfish love that does not expect anything in return.

These five Greek words for love aid us in describing the five ways of loving that should exist in a solid marriage. One of these loves probably played a role in your initial relationship with your spouse. Most likely, one of these loves is neglected within your marriage. The love, however, that holds a marriage together is *agapé* love! This is the love that should dominate our preaching and shepherding ministry!

> *But speaking the truth in love, [we] may grow up into Him in all things, which is the head, even Christ:* – Ephesians 4:15

Preach Love!

> *And now abideth faith, hope, charity, these three; but the greatest of these is charity.* — 1 Corinthians 13:13

Essayist and poet Henry David Thoreau, who was made famous through his book *Walden*, wrote: "The mass of men lead lives of quiet desperation." He may have put his finger on where most of our listening audience live their lives. Thus, I intentionally focus on 1 Corinthians 13:13 as my text again. Some preachers will wax bold preaching about *faith*, but only as they define it in their system of theology! Others will offer *hope*, but with little practical application. But what those lives need is *love* – to know that they are loved by someone, by God!

Agapé love was the theme of Jesus' preaching. When a scribe challenged Jesus concerning which law was the most important among the over 600 laws of the Jews, Jesus answered in Mark 12:29-32: *The first of all the commandments is, Hear, O Israel; The Lord our God is one Lord: And thou shalt love the Lord thy God with all thy heart, and with all thy soul, and with all thy mind, and with all thy strength: this is the first commandment. And the second is like, namely this, Thou shalt love thy neighbor as thyself. There is none other commandment greater than these.*

Perhaps, John, the apostle whom Jesus loved, understood the thrust of Jesus' ministry more than all the others! (See John 13:34; 15:9-13; 3:16.) Did the apostles truly capture the emphasis of Jesus' preaching and ministry?

To answer that question, let me draw your attention to the difference in ministry and preaching approaches between *eros* and *agapé* loves. The great Methodist missionary, E. Stanley Jones, in *Christian Maturity*, draws the following distinctions:

Eros	*Agapé*
Eros is acquisitive longing.	*Agapé* is sacrificial giving
Eros is an upward movement.	*Agapé* is a downward movement.
Eros is man's way to God.	*Agapé* is God's way to man.
Eros is man's effort. It assumes that man's salvation is his own work.	*Agapé* is God's grace. Salvation is the work of Divine love.
Eros is egocentric love, a form of self-assertion of the highest, noblest, sublimest kind.	*Agapé* is unselfish love, it "seeketh not its own," it gives itself away.
Eros seeks to gain its life, a life divine, immortalized.	*Agapé* lives the life of God, therefore dares to "lose it."
Eros is the will to get and possess which depends on man's want and need.	*Agapé* is freedom in giving, which depends on God's wealth and plenty.
Eros is primarily man's love; God is the object of *Eros*. Even when it is attributed to God, *Eros* is patterned on human love.	*Agapé* is primarily God's love; God is *Agapé*. Even when it is attributed to man, *Agapé* is patterned on Divine love.

Eros	*Agapé*
Eros is determined by the quality, the beauty and worth of its object. It is not spontaneous, but "evoked" or "motivated."	*Agapé* is sovereign in relation to its object and directed to both "the evil and the good." It is spontaneous, "overflowing," or "unmotivated."
Eros recognizes value in its object – and loves it.	*Agapé* loves – and creates value in its object.
Eros is trying to reach God – a struggle.	*Agapé* is God reaching man – a surrender.
Eros is based upon attainments – man's merit.	*Agapé* is based upon obtainment – God's gift.
Eros makes religion a demand upon the will.	*Agapé* makes the relationship a surrender of the will.
Eros is exhaustive.	*Agapé* is inexhaustible.
Eros looks for a return and is disappointed if it does not come.	*Agapé* asks for nothing but the privilege of giving itself and gets everything in return.

All religious systems and all life line up on one side or the other of these two types of love. Scriptural conversion is the conversion of our loves! We move from *eros* love to *agapé* love! *Eros* love ascends from the human to the Divine and forms an egocentric religion. *Eros* is self-centered! *Eros* is sub-Christian love! On the other hand, *agapé* love condescends from the Divine to the human and forms a theocentric relationship. *Agapé* is self-giving! *Agapé* is Christian love! Again, love is the basic need within Man and should be the basic theme of our preaching! It was for Jesus! And it was for His disciples! Observe Paul in 1 Corinthians 13:13; James in James 2:5 and 8; Peter in 2 Peter 1:1-11; and John in 1 John 4:7-21. Yes, the disciples got it! But have we?

> *Beloved, let us love one another: for love is of God; and every one that loveth is born of God, and knoweth God.*
> *– 1 John 4:7*

Avoid the Single Worst Mistake in Preaching

> *Not as though I had already attained, either were already perfect: but I follow after, if that I may apprehend that for which also I am apprehended of Christ Jesus. Brethren, I count not myself to have apprehended: but this one thing I do, forgetting those things which are behind, and reaching forth unto those things which are before, I press toward the mark for the prize of the high calling of God in Christ Jesus.*
> — Philippians 3:12-14

Perhaps the worst mistake a preacher can make is to think that he has already attained, is already perfect, and is already mature! The preacher should never feel that he is spiritually mature — to think like that demonstrates immaturity! When the preacher enters the auditorium, looks around at the congregation, and, then, entertains the thought that he is the most spiritually mature person in the room, he is already defeated as the preacher for the hour!

Oh, the preacher may think that he has more Bible knowledge, has obtained a degree or two after his name, and has gained the high position of pastor, but he makes a mistake in thinking that he may be more mature or better equipped than others that sit before him!

I recall years ago an elderly deacon sharing with me that he usually reads the Bible through each year ten times or more. Over his lifetime, he had read the Bible through hundreds of times, and a volume of memorized Bible verses confirmed that he was sincere. Then he shared with me that he gave himself a project of reading the Bible backward to see if he had missed anything! How would it be possible for my sermon to challenge that man? On another occasion, I came to a church to preach on prayer only to be introduced to a blind, elderly woman who was the intercessor in the church. I immediately sensed that I needed to learn about prayer from her! Humbling experiences, indeed!

John the Baptist was one of the least educated and least refined preachers during the time of Jesus, but he humbled himself and said that he needed to decrease before Jesus and that he was not worthy even to lace up His shoes. But he did possess one unmatched quality that others lacked. He was filled with the Spirit of God. Recognizing this quality, Jesus said of John the Baptist that he was the greatest in the long line of prophets and that there was none greater than he!

The Apostle Paul stated in 2 Corinthians 4:5, *For we preach not ourselves, but Christ Jesus the Lord; and ourselves your servants for Jesus' sake.* Paul did not lift himself up before his audience. Instead, he lifted up Jesus!

The goal of discipleship preaching is not to reach a point of deceiving ourselves into thinking that we have arrived as mature believers or mature preachers. The goal is to be as Spirit-filled as possible and to preach the truth in love. May we press toward that prize in our high calling!

> *Whosoever therefore shall humble himself as this little child, the same is greatest in the kingdom of heaven.*
> – Matthew 18:4

Sounding Brass and Tinkling Cymbals or Trailing Tears?

> *Though I speak with the tongues of men and of angels, and have not charity, I am become as sounding brass, or a tinkling cymbal. And though I have the gift of prophecy, and understand all mysteries, and all knowledge; and though I have all faith, so that I could remove mountains, and have not charity, I am nothing.* — 1 Corinthians 13:1-2

How will those who listen to our preaching remember us? How will the Lord, Who listens and discerns our hearts, remember us? Will it be our oratory skills like that of great preachers or even of angels? The Apostle Paul wrote that without love, we are like sounding brass or tinkling cymbals! He was right! We might be able to explain the great prophecies, expound grand doctrines, or extol the grappling mysteries of Christianity, but without love, we are nothing and say nothing!

Ask any believer to quote a memorized Bible verse, and you may hear John 3:16, *For God so loved...*, or perhaps from the lazy, John 11:35, *Jesus wept.* Those two verses are not necessarily disconnected! Jesus so loved that He was often moved with compassion. He was moved to tears! Hebrews 5:7 states concerning Jesus, *Who in the days of His flesh, when He had offered up prayers and supplications with strong crying and tears unto Him that was able to save Him from death, and was heard in that He feared.* When Jesus asked His disciples who the people thought He was, they stated that some felt that He was like Jeremiah, the great Weeping Prophet (Matthew 16:14)!

Over the entombed Lazarus, Jesus wept! Over the embattled city of Jerusalem, Jesus wept! Over the impending crucifixion, Jesus wept! In Psalm 56:8, God states that He saves our tears in a bottle and records them in a book. Perhaps, one day, God the Father will show us the bottle of Jesus' tears and the tearful notes inscribed in a book! On Jesus' last night on earth, most likely, He was placed in the bottle-shaped dungeon below Caiaphas' house awaiting the morning's crucifixion. Powerful, isn't it, the symbolism?!

While John the Baptist was the voice of one crying in the wilderness with a message that sounded like a funeral dirge, Jesus was the voice of one speaking love with a message that sounded like a wedding dance! (See Matthew 11:17.) Funerals and weddings are both emotional times of tears!

There is a story of the Apostle John in his last days when he was too feeble to walk or preach. His followers would bring him into the assembly upon a pallet, and he would share his message, "My beloved, love one another." That was his "pallet message" – the one that he is remembered preaching. What is your "pallet message"? Note the famed preachers and a message for which they are remembered:
- ☐ Robert Murray McCheyne, *Love of Christ* (2 Corinthians 5:14)
- ☐ George Müller, *Behold, What Manner of Love* (1 John 3:1-3)
- ☐ D. Martyn Lloyd-Jones, *The Breadth, Length, Depth, Height of God's Love* (Ephesians 3:15-19)
- ☐ Charles Spurgeon, *The Drawings of Divine Love* (John 6:44)
- ☐ George Truett, *Love's Delays* (John 11:6)
- ☐ T. DeWitt Talmage, *The Ministry of Tears* (Revelation 7:17)

In 1 Corinthians 13, Paul challenged his readers, including us today, to have a ministry of love. We should pray and preach with a broken heart! Impacted by my prayers through a passage of Scripture in preparation to preach, I often find myself so emotionally moved while preaching that I am brought to tears! In times of devotion and times of desperation, I find myself speechless in my prayers, but with these groaning words, "Oh, God, see my tears!"

> *And we have known and believed the love that God hath to us. God is love; and he that dwelleth in love dwelleth in God, and God in him.* – 1 John 4:16

Conclusion

the whole counsel of God

*For I have not shunned to declare unto you
all the counsel of God.* — Acts 20:27

CHAPTER 9

As a young preacher, I often heard older men speak about preaching the "whole counsel of God." I wondered at the time, how could mere man preach the whole counsel of God and just how long would this take?

Carl Wilson, in his book *With Christ in the School of Disciple Building*, shares how Jesus used a three-year, hands-on method of discipling His followers. He then, correctly, points out how the Apostle Paul declared in Acts 20 that over the course of three years, he delivered to the Ephesian believers the whole counsel of God! The discipleship principles and methodology given to the Disciples by Jesus were now being passed on again to other disciples.

In this book we have sought to deliver Christ's discipleship insights which consist of a progressive series of steps that encompass the essentials of God's counsel. These successive steps were first revealed by God the Father to the Israelites in the Feasts of the Lord. Jesus, as God's Son, taught the twelve disciples these same successive steps over the course of three years. Then the Holy Spirit, through His inspiration, led the Early Church to embrace this discipleship process as revealed by Paul at Ephesus and further in the writings of the apostles.

Let us review these steps and ask ourselves, do we as preachers in the Twenty-First Century preach the whole counsel of God?

Salvation: *What do I need to know and do to be saved?*
- Topics to be taught:
  - ☐ God
  - ☐ Sin
  - ☐ Repentance
  - ☐ Faith
  - ☐ Man
  - ☐ Satan
  - ☐ The Fall
  - ☐ Creation
  - ☐ The Gospel
  - ☐ Assurance
  - ☐ Heaven and Hell
- **Key Books:** 1 John; Romans

Separation: *How can I overcome temptations and trials?*
- Topics to be taught:
  - ☐ Enlightenment
  - ☐ Regeneration
  - ☐ Personal Sins
  - ☐ Satanic Snares
  - ☐ Moral Absolutes
  - ☐ Witnessing
  - ☐ Baptism
- **Key Books:** James; Galatians

Surrender: *Is the Bible relevant and trustworthy?*
- Topics to be taught:
  - ☐ Ministry Training
  - ☐ Lordship of Christ
  - ☐ Prayer

- ☐ Stewardship
- ☐ Tithe
- ☐ Ambitions
- ☐ Will of God
- ☐ Relationships
- **Key Books:** 1 and 2 Thessalonians; 2 Peter; Jude; 1 and 2 Corinthians

---

Spirit-control: *How can I live the Christian life?*

- Topics to be taught:
  - ☐ Leadership Development
  - ☐ Trinity
  - ☐ Holy Spirit
  - ☐ Sovereignty of God
  - ☐ Prophecy
  - ☐ Gifts of the Spirit
  - ☐ Call to Service
  - ☐ Role of Angels
- **Key Books:** Ephesians; 1 Timothy

Suffering: *How do I make sense of suffering as a Christian?*

- Topics to be taught:
  - ☐ Re-evaluation
  - ☐ Perseverance
  - ☐ Providence
  - ☐ Trust
  - ☐ Warfare
  - ☐ Sacrifice
- **Key Books:** 1 Peter; 2 Timothy

Sensitivity: *How do I serve and pray for others who are hurting?*

- Topics to be taught:
  - ☐ Participation and Delegation
  - ☐ Christian Works
  - ☐ Church
  - ☐ Judaism
  - ☐ Kingdoms of God and Satan
  - ☐ Cosmology
- **Key Books:** Philippians; Titus; Philemon; 3 John

Spirituality: *What is the goal of the Christian life?*

- Topics to be taught:
  - ☐ Exchanged Life
  - ☐ Sanctification
  - ☐ Fruitfulness
  - ☐ Love
  - ☐ Judgment
  - ☐ Death
  - ☐ Second Coming
- **Key Books:** Colossians; Hebrews

Certainly, other topics and books of the Bible may be utilized, but, from my perspective, these are the indispensable ones that must be included.

> *Therefore watch, and remember, that by the space of three years I ceased not to warn every one night and day with tears.* – Acts 20:31

Paul's Preaching Pledge

But as we were allowed of God to be put in trust with the gospel, even so we speak... — 1 Thessalonians 2:4

Paul's pledge – my pledge, and prayerfully your pledge – is to be faithful in preaching! In 1 Thessalonians 2, the apostle declares multiple aspects of his pledge to be a good steward of the Gospel entrusted to his care. Biblical preaching is different from all other forms of communication, for to a certain degree the Holy Spirit seeks to speak through His called messengers. Because of that stewardship, we must respond by being faithful. May we explore the various aspects of Paul's "Preaching Pledge" and evaluate our commitment to that aspect of our own preaching.

Paul's Preaching Excluded Popular Approaches

For yourselves, brethren, know our entrance in unto you, that it was not in vain: But even after that we had suffered before, and were shamefully entreated, as ye know, at Philippi, we were bold in our God to speak unto you the gospel of God with much contention. For our exhortation was not of deceit, nor of uncleanness, nor in guile: But as we were allowed of God to be put in trust with the gospel, even so we speak; not as pleasing men, but God, which trieth our hearts. For neither at any time used we flattering words, as ye know, nor a cloke of covetousness; God is witness: Nor of men sought we glory, neither of you, nor yet of others, when we might have been burdensome, as the apostles of Christ.
— 1 Thessalonians 2:1-6

- ☐ Paul's Preaching did not contain error: *not of deceit* (verse 3).
- ☐ Paul's Preaching did not contain impurity: *not of uncleanness* (verse 3).

- ☐ Paul's Preaching did not contain trickery: *nor in guile* (verse 3).
- ☐ Paul's Preaching was not men-pleasing: *not as pleasing men* (verse 4).
- ☐ Paul's Preaching was not a pretext for greed: *nor a cloke of covetousness* (verse 5).
- ☐ Paul's Preaching was not for personal glory: *nor of men sought we glory* (verse 6).

I dare say that among the many preachers in Christianity today, there are few who have fully taken Paul's Preaching Pledge to avoid the pitfalls that have become popular approaches to preaching. In how many of these six pitfalls have you found yourself? Will you join Paul in making a fresh pledge to exclude them from your preaching?

Paul's Preaching Alluded to Positive Approaches

> *But we were gentle among you, even as a nurse cherisheth her children: So being affectionately desirous of you, we were willing to have imparted unto you, not the gospel of God only, but also our own souls, because ye were dear unto us. For ye remember, brethren, our labour and travail: for labouring night and day, because we would not be chargeable unto any of you, we preached unto you the gospel of God. Ye are witnesses, and God also, how holily and justly and unblameably we behaved ourselves among you that believe: As ye know how we exhorted and comforted and charged every one of you, as a father doth his children, That ye would walk worthy of God, who hath called you unto His kingdom and glory.*
> – 1 Thessalonians 2:7-12

Paul's pledge to be faithful in preaching moves from negative to positive comments in this second section of 1 Thessalonians 2. It is never enough to dwell on the things we should not do in our preaching. We should also consider the positive instructions. Here, the apostle uses two illustrations to make his point: our pastoring and our preaching should be as a *nursing mother* and a *nurturing father:*

Paul's preaching came as a nursing mother: *we were gentle among you, even as a nurse cherisheth her children* (verse 7). The Apostle Paul stated that he did not come unto the Thessalonians as one requiring honor and demanding certain privileges or perks. Instead, Paul said that he came as a nursing mother desiring to comfort, to nourish, and to love the Thessalonians. Paul used warm words of affection and care. Paul's motivation is set at variance against many of today's pastors who seek the perks of a senior pastor and demand one benefit after another from the congregation – vacations, 401Ks, book money, days off to play golf, etc. Setting themselves upon a pedestal of importance and privilege, they unfortunately distance themselves from those to whom they are to minister. Paul's use of the nursing mother pictures someone who is exhausted from laboring to meet the domestic demands. In Deuteronomy 22:6, the Hebrews pictured such devotion by that of a mother bird sitting long hours upon her eggs, keeping them warm and protected.

Paul's preaching came as a nurturing father: *we exhorted and comforted and charged every one of you, as a father doth his children* (verse 11). Fathers have a different role to play in the raising of children. While the mother offers emotional stability as a caregiver, the father offers strong counsel, exhortation, discipline and structure to the home. In our text, the father encouraged the children to stay the course in their purposeful calling. The father's role is to shape the future of the children as he discerns their created purpose, giftedness, and abilities. Likewise, the pastor should shape a congregation in the desired course based upon their called purpose, giftedness, and abilities within the congregation. No two churches are the same. The pastor should discover the uniqueness of his congregation.

The Apostle Paul is right on target in his instructions. Pastors are to be as a nursing mother and as a nurturing father in ministering and preaching tenderly to their congregations! If this were the approach of pastors today, much of the contention, strife, and division would be alleviated. And the churches would be growing, not disappearing!

Paul's Preaching Included Prescribed Approaches

For this cause also thank we God without ceasing, because, when ye received the word of God which ye heard of us, ye received it not as the word of men, but as it is in truth, the word of God, which effectually worketh also in you that believe. For ye, brethren, became followers of the churches of God which in Judaea are in Christ Jesus: for ye also have suffered like things of your own countrymen, even as they have of the Jews: Who both killed the Lord Jesus, and their own prophets, and have persecuted us; and they please not God, and are contrary to all men: Forbidding us to speak to the Gentiles that they might be saved, to fill up their sins alway: for the wrath is come upon them to the uttermost.
– 1 Thessalonians 2:13-16

As we continue to explore Paul's pledge to be faithful in preaching, we discover four simple, but powerful principles. Paul envisioned these principles to be straightforwardly applied to the preaching of the Gospel. Again, his prescribed approach to preaching resonates down through the centuries, even down to our day!

Paul's preaching was in the Holy Spirit with much assurance: *For our gospel came not unto you in word only, but also in power, and in the Holy Ghost, and in much assurance* (chapter 1 verse 5). Our proclamation should come from the Holy Spirit as He motivates and inspires both the message and the manner of delivery. This is without exception! The Spirit's anointing is essential to preaching. Brethren, preach with power through the Spirit's anointing!

Paul's preaching originated from his prayer time: *For this cause also thank we God without ceasing* (verse 13). Our proclamation should come from our intimacy in prayer. Having heard from the Lord in prayer, we then have a message to preach, but not before then! Too many preachers today are preaching from the Internet, a set of commentaries, or even sermon outline books. These tools may be helpful, but none are a substitute for prayer! Brethren, preach from your prayer closet!

Paul's preaching was faithful to the Word of God: *the word of God which ye heard of us, ye received it not as the word of men, but as it is in truth, the word of God* (verse 13). Our message and stories will soon vanish as the morning dew. God's message is, however, eternal and will return with much fruit! Brethren, preach the eternal Word of God!

Paul's preaching was bold, even as he counted the cost: *...ye also have suffered like things of your own countrymen, even as they have of the Jews: Who both killed the Lord Jesus, and their own prophets, and have persecuted us; and they please not God, and are contrary to all men: Forbidding us to speak to the Gentiles that they might be saved, to fill up their sins alway: for the wrath is come upon them to the uttermost* (verses 14-16). Jesus was said to be meek, but not weak. Neither should we be weak! Our preaching should be strong and bold, fearless. What can man do to someone who has risen from his knees, empowered by the Holy Spirit, and proclaims the Word of God? Brethren, preach boldly with much assurance!

With great precision the Apostle Paul summarized the priorities of preaching in four simple statements! These statements formed the New Testament principles upon which Paul preached and are the prescribed approaches for today's preacher!

Paul's Preaching Concluded with Personal Approaches

> *But we, brethren, being taken from you for a short time in presence, not in heart, endeavoured the more abundantly to see your face with great desire. Wherefore we would have come unto you, even I Paul, once and again; but Satan hindered us. For what is our hope, or joy, or crown of rejoicing? Are not even ye in the presence of our Lord Jesus Christ at His coming? For ye are our glory and joy.*
> – 1 Thessalonians 2:17-20

Finally, Paul appealed to his personal involvement with his readers. He had invested time and effort to win them to Christ and to disciple them. Although now physically removed from them, he appealed yet once again to his personal contact with his readers.

Paul's preaching appealed personally to the brethren: *But we, brethren, being taken from you for a short time in presence, not in heart, endeavoured the more abundantly to see your face with great desire* (verse 17). Paul longed to see those whom he had discipled face to face and to minister compassion upon them. In order to be personal with the brethren and the congregation, the pastor must know his people. He must be with them through visitation, hospital care, funeral opportunities, and crisis intervention. Sadly, today our congregations are weakened by our tendency to have assistants, not the preacher, minister in times of crisis.

Paul's preaching rejoiced in the presence of those with whom he invested the truth: *But we, brethren, being taken from you for a short time in presence, not in heart, endeavoured the more abundantly to see your face with great desire* (verse 17). In addition, the Apostle Paul expressed his desire to once again see for himself the fruit of his labors in the lives of those whom he nurtured. The pastor's investment of truth should be nurtured through discipleship. The impact of nurturing grows deeper over time, and should continue even when new opportunities separate the pastor from his congregation.

Paul's preaching overcame Satan's attempts to hinder his preaching: *Wherefore we would have come unto you, even I Paul, once and again; but Satan hindered us* (verse 18). The apostle was constantly opposed in his preaching! Pastoring and preaching truth invites Satan's opposition. Satan will often use people, trials, and temptations to oppose the pastor who will boldly preach God's Word. His attacks will at times seem relentless as Satan delights in wearing down the saints and, for this reason, the pastor should not grow weary in well doing.

Paul's preaching expresses hope, joy, and rejoicing: *For what is our hope, or joy, or crown of rejoicing? Are not even ye in the presence of our Lord Jesus Christ at His coming? For ye are our glory and joy* (verses 19-20). Lastly, Paul pledged to fill his preaching with hope and joy with the prospects of the crown of rejoicing to those who overcome. He pledged to avoid constant negativity and condemnation. Instead, he disciplined himself to produce preaching that was uplifting and edifying.

In review, Paul has pledged that his approach to preaching would:

- ☐ exclude the more popular approaches to preaching
- ☐ be positive
- ☐ follow a prescription laid out in Scripture
- ☐ and be personal.

Brother, review for a few minutes each of the four parts to Paul's commitment. Then respond with your heart to the apostle's challenge to be faithful to Biblical preaching. Will you, too, pledge yourself to such a challenge?

> *...The word is near you, even in your mouth and in your heart. It is the secret of faith, which is the burden of our preaching,...*
> – Romans 10:8 (Phillips)

The Completed Challenge

> *Wherefore I will not be negligent to put you always in remembrance of these things, though ye know them, and be established in the present truth.* – 2 Peter 1:12

The use of the number seven in Scripture always symbolizes completion. We have examined individually each of the seven God-ordained steps of discipleship that should shape our preaching, but it is now time to examine the complete picture of all 7 of these indispensable truths.

Step #1 – A Life Message Initiated by Salvation

> *Now therefore arise, O LORD God, into thy resting place, Thou, and the ark of Thy strength: let Thy priests, O LORD God, be clothed with salvation, and let Thy saints rejoice in goodness.* – 2 Chronicles 6:41

Our starting position is one of personal salvation. Without a conversion experience, we will be empty men preaching a toothless Gospel! The Apostle Paul challenges the preacher in 2 Corinthians 13:5: *Examine yourselves, whether ye be in the faith; prove your own selves. Know ye not your own selves, how that Jesus Christ is in you, except ye be reprobates?*

Step #2 – A Life Message Interpreted Through Separation

> *I have preached righteousness in the great congregation: lo, I have not refrained my lips, O LORD, Thou knows.*
> – Psalm 40:9

Clearly God desires His servants to live out their salvation in a life of separation. As 2 Corinthians 6:17 reads: *Wherefore come out from among them, and be ye separate, saith the Lord, and touch not the unclean thing; and I will receive you.* God unquestionably has called us unto a life of holiness in all and every area of conversation (1 Peter 1:15).

Step #3 – A Life Message Integrated Through Surrender

> *Study to show thyself approved unto God, a workman that needeth not to be ashamed rightly dividing the word of truth.*
> – 2 Timothy 2:15

It is not enough merely to hear the Word, we need to be doers also (James 1:22). God's Word must be effectually worked out in our lives as we surrender to the truths we have both read and heard (1 Thessalonians 2:13; Philippians 2:12). Thus, we should hold fast to the form of the sound words of faith and love (1 Timothy 1:13).

Step #4 – A Life Message Inspired by the Spirit

> *The Spirit of the Lord is upon Me, because He hath anointed Me to preach the gospel...* – Luke 4:18a

Our preaching must not be of enticing words of our own making, but in a demonstration of the Spirit and of power (1Corinthians 2:4). As Zechariah 4:6 reminds us: *This is the word of the LORD..., saying, Not by might, nor by power, but by My spirit, saith the LORD of hosts.* Our preaching must be Spirit-anointed!

Step #5 – A Life Message Illuminated by Suffering

> *Notwithstanding the Lord stood with me, and strengthened me; that by me the preaching might be fully known, and that all the Gentiles might hear: and I was delivered out of the mouth of the lion.* – 2 Timothy 4:17

Peter reminds us in 1 Peter 2:20 that we should be patient in suffering for this is acceptable to God! Through suffering, the preacher will gain a position of empathy wherein he may be able to minister more effectively to his congregation (Philippians 4:12)!

Step #6 – A Life Message Intensified to Sensitivity

> *Preach the word: be instant in season, and out of season; reprove, rebuke, exhort with all long suffering and doctrine. But watch thou in all things, endure afflictions, do the work of an evangelist, make full proof of thy ministry.*
> – 2 Timothy 4:2, 5

The preacher must transfer the message to faithful men (2 Timothy 2:2). He should not be looking out after his own needs as much as the needs of others to whom he ministers (Philippians 2:3).

Step #7 – A Life Message Incarnated into Spirituality

> *But speaking the truth in love, [we] may grow up into Him in all things, which is the head, even Christ:* – Ephesians 4:15

The goal in preaching is to be able to present every man perfect in Christ Jesus (Colossians 1:28). In doing so, our message is clearly love (1 Corinthians 13:13).

Dear Brother, you have been called as a preacher of God's Word. Your preaching has now been freshly challenged by His Word. Will you faithfully be committed to His Word as a tool to regularly disciple through your preaching?

> *If thou put the brethren in remembrance of these things, thou shalt be a good minister of Jesus Christ, nourished up in the words of faith and of good doctrine, whereunto thou hast attained.* – 1 Timothy 4:6

Spiritual Maturity Requires Finishing Strong

> *And it came to pass, when Jesus had finished all these sayings, He said unto His disciples,...* — Matthew 26:1

Matthew records that when Jesus had finished all His teaching, He still had work to do with His disciples. Recently, the wife of a pastor friend passed away after 60 years of marriage and ministry. Before she died, she turned to her husband and said, "Finish the work." What a tremendous challenge to each of us in the ministry. Even if our Completer is gone, let us finish the work. Was this not the challenge to Joshua after Moses departed or to Elisha after Elijah was taken up?

I often hear pastors say, "Each Monday I would resign, but my wife won't let me!" Or, "If it weren't for people, I would enjoy the pastorate." Oh, the temptation to burn out and quit before the work is finished! But spiritual maturity that is produced by love requires the greatest sacrifice of laying down one's life for another (John 15:13). Whether it involves enduring the daily death of the hardships of pastoring or continuing to minister in the midst of physical limitations that demand retirement, may we join Paul by keeping the faith as we finish our course (2 Timothy 4:7). Let us not burn out but finish strong! Let us have an exit strategy of finishing! May we:

- ☐ **Love compassionately:** *These things I command you, that ye love one another.* – John 15:17
- ☐ **Teach continually:** *Preach the word; be instant in season, out of season,....* – 2 Timothy 4:2
- ☐ **Walk circumspectly:** *See then that ye walk circumspectly, not as fools, but as wise.* – Ephesians 5:15
- ☐ **Listen cautiously:** *Blessed is the man that walketh not in the counsel of the ungodly, nor standeth in the way of sinners, nor sitteth in the seat of the scornful.* – Psalm 1:1
- ☐ **Live consistently:** *If we live in the Spirit, let us also walk in the Spirit.* – Galatians 5:25

As a pastor I installed a "deacon rotating system" wherein a deacon would serve three years and then step aside for at least a year. I had one deacon obstinately resist the idea. When I visited him, he challenged me with this question, "Bro. Rob, what would you do if we initiated a pastor rotating system?" I responded, "Well, I would keep loving my wife and family. I would continue having my daily quiet time of prayer and Bible study. I would still witness to the lost. I also would seek to live a separated lifestyle. I would also preach as the occasion was presented. In fact, not much would change in my life for I was doing these things before the church ever called me to pastor!" What if, at the end of my life, I am unable to pastor? What will I do? Finish strong!

When Jesus announced on the cross that it was finished (the atoning payment for sin was paid in full (John 19:30)), He still had some work to do: be buried, rise from the dead, restore and commission the disciples, ascend to the Father, send the Holy Spirit to establish the Church, and ever live to make intercession for us! Yes, He still had work to do! But in this life, He finished strong!

> *Now before the feast of the passover, when Jesus knew that His hour was come that He should depart out of this world unto the Father, having loved His own which were in the world, He loved them unto the end.*   – John 13:1

Resources

The resources listed have been utilized in gaining insights in writing and teaching the material from this book. These resources, however, do not necessarily mean a 100 percent endorsement of the contents of each book. As Dr. R.G. Lee told me when I was going to the seminary, "You should go as a cow!" I hesitated to ask what was meant by that comment, not wanting to appear stupid, but I did ask what he meant. Dr. Lee said, "A cow knows what to eat in the field, has enough sense not to eat some things, and to spit out still others!"

Secret#1 A Life-Message Initiated by Salvation

- ☐ Rob Finley, *Recapturing Biblical Intercession*
- ☐ Andrew Murray, *Helps to Intercession*
- ☐ A.T. Pierson, *Lessons in the School of Prayer*
- ☐ Andrew Murray, *How to Raise your Children for Christ*

Secret#2 A Life-Message Interpreted Through Separation

- ☐ E.M. Bounds, *Power Through Prayer*
- ☐ E.M. Bounds, *Powerful and Prayerful Pulpits*
- ☐ Stephen Olford, *A Way of Holiness*
- ☐ Gregory Frizzell, *Returning to Holiness*

Secret #3 A Life-Message Integrated Through Surrender

- ☐ John Phillips, *Exploring the Scriptures*
- ☐ John Phillips, *Bible Explorer's Guide*
- ☐ David Olford, *A Passion for Preaching*
- ☐ E.W. Bullinger, *Figures of Speech Uses in the Bible*
- ☐ Stephen Olford, *Anointed Expository Preaching*

Secret #4 A Life-Message Inspired by the Spirit

- ☐ Bertha Smith, *How the Spirit Filled my Life*
- ☐ Stephen Olford, *Tabernacle, Camping with God*
- ☐ W.A. Criswell, *The Baptism, Filling and Gifts of the Holy Spirit*

Secret #5 A Life-Message Illuminated by Suffering

- ☐ Stephen Olford, *The Sword of Suffering*
- ☐ Manley Beasley, *Alive by His Faith*
- ☐ Paul Billheimer, *Destined for the Throne*
- ☐ Arthur Mathews, *Born for Battle*
- ☐ Paul Billheimer, *Don't Waste Your Sorrows*

Secret #6 A Life-Message Intensified to Sensitivity

- ☐ Oswald J. Smith, *Spiritual Leadership*
- ☐ Ron Owens, *Return to Worship*
- ☐ Carl Wilson, *With Christ in the School of Disciple Building*

Secret #7 A Life-Message Incarnated into Spirituality

- ☐ E. Stanley Jones, *Christian Maturity*
- ☐ Ed Wheat, *Love Life*
- ☐ James G. Lawson, *Deeper Experiences of Famous Christians*

Prayer Resources

www.PrayerResources.org

Prayer Resources, Inc. is a Christian ministry designed to serve as a resource to the Body of Christ in the arena of prayer and spiritual awakening. Founded by Rob and Judy Finley in 1985 and originally based in Memphis, TN, the ministry has reached into multiple denominations both in the US and abroad.

As president, author, and primary speaker for Prayer Resources, **Dr Rob Finley** has conducted over 1000 meetings. His educational training includes degrees from Rhodes College, Southwestern Baptist Theological Seminary, and Luther Rice Seminary. His ministerial experience as a pastor of Southern Baptist churches for 12 years and teaching Bible in Christian schools for seven years has provided a thorough command of Scripture capably communicated in both pulpit and teaching forums. He has authored the encompassing manual on prayer entitled *Recapturing Biblical Intercession*, as well as *Recapturing the Biblical Epic of Prayer* and a six week preparation guide entitled *Meditations for Revival*, based on the 42 parables of Jesus. He has also written articles for several Christian periodicals.

Judy Finley serves as author, speaker, and administrator for Prayer Resources. She has studied with her husband throughout his education. Her experience as a pastor's wife and as a group leader in Bible Study Fellowship for 10 years has equipped her in the field of counseling women and speaking at women's conferences.

Now in semi-retirement, the Finleys continue to work together in writing and material development for Prayer Resources through both publications and a weekly blog for pastors. They currently reside on their daughter's farm in Cayce, KY, and maintain an active discipling role for their two married daughters, their husbands, six grandchildren, and a great grand-daughter.

If you enjoyed this book, please tell others…

- ☐ Post a 5-star review on Amazon.
- ☐ Write about the book on your Facebook, Twitter, Instagram, LinkedIn, or any social media platforms you regularly use.
- ☐ If you blog, consider referencing the book or publishing an excerpt from the book with a link back to our websites. You have permission to do this as long as you provide proper credit and backlinks.
- ☐ Recommend the book to pastors—word-of-mouth is still the most effective form of advertising.
- ☐ Purchase additional copies to give away to all the pastors in your life.
- ☐ Learn more about the authors or contact them at www.PrayerResources.org

www.ingramcontent.com/pod-product-compliance
Lightning Source LLC
Chambersburg PA
CBHW072018110526
44592CB00012B/1356